Girls, Let's Talk About Relationships and Sex

A Simple Guide to Get You Through Your Teenage Years

Darcey M. Wyatt with
Drew Winters

Table of Contents

Acknowledgements

A huge thanks to a fellow author Drew Winters who collaborated with me on this book. He is a brilliant author and colleague who brought the male aspects of relationships and sex, to enable us to write a thoroughly rounded book on this subject for the girls. We also collaborated on a similar book for boys: *Guys, Let's Talk About Relationships and Sex* for the same reasons.

To our families who patiently got on with their lives while we spent hours together writing this book to get the messages out there to the wonderful teenagers who deserve to know more about themselves and their friends. To take onboard the information, be empowered and put it into practice to lead the lives they want to live.

Foreword

We wrote this book for teenage girls to understand and be empowered with good information to get through the tough teenage years. Finding out about relationships and sex at an early age is important as the teenage years have a huge impact on their mental and emotional health.

We have worked in the education system for many years and have seen kids struggling with so many issues. A book to read of their own giving reasons for why and how they may feel can be found in these pages.

This book covers sexual and emotional health, safety and respect for others and also acknowledges that as a teenage girl, they have a voice that should be listened to and heard.

After each chapter, there are pages to write any notes, comments, thoughts, feelings or anything you want. Sometimes it's good to get it out.

Girls, Let's Talk About Relationships and Sex can be read from beginning to end (there is so much stuff in there) or by going directly to relevant chapters. Your choice Girls – because you need to make informed choices about your life. Start now, you are in safe hands with the information in this book.

Darcey Wyatt & Drew M Winters

Introduction

Going through puberty as a young girl is so confusing. This monster invades your body, changes things, and makes things grow, and no one tells you what's going on. –Katharine Isabelle

Being a girl is hard. You enter your teen years and your whole world is turned upside down and inside out whether you like it or not. This period of your life is known as *puberty* and it can be terrifying, especially as a young girl whose body is changing so dramatically. You also face pressure from peers, society, and men to become sexually active once you become a teen, even if you aren't emotionally or mentally ready.

The birth rate for teens in 2020 was 15.4 births for every 1,000 females aged between 15 to 19, with a total of 158,043 births to the girls in this group (OASH, 2020: par. 3). The United States has been found to have one of the highest teen pregnancy rates in the world due to various reasons, including those sexually active teenagers who don't use contraceptives have a 90% chance of becoming pregnant within a year of engaging in sexual activities (*11 Facts about teen pregnancy*, 2015: par. 10).

Sex and puberty are awkward and uncomfortable topics that few adults want to discuss with their children. But that doesn't mean you don't have questions. Sexual grooming, online predators, sexual assault, and rape are the realities that most young girls have to face in daily life, regardless of their age. This danger often increases due to a lack of knowledge about the changes that accompany puberty, what a healthy relationship really is, and how to engage in safe sex if you are mentally and emotionally ready. This is why you need to understand what puberty is and how it can affect you, what your rights are, how the law can protect you, and what measures you can take to keep yourself safe without being ashamed of growing up into a young woman.

There's a lot of conflicting and inaccurate information available online, opening you up to the dangers of online predators and seeing things you're not mentally or emotionally ready for. Learning about and understanding what healthy and happy relationships look like is also more important than ever, especially if you don't see examples of such relationships in your daily life. Taking care of your developing body is often overlooked too, but it's so important! Especially if you don't have a mother figure in your life who can safely guide you through these changes.

For most of my career, I have worked with parents and children, supporting their learning through the training of teachers, tutors, and support staff. I have also worked in primary and secondary schools, as well as in a communication college for young people with learning difficulties. My career and experiences as a mother of two children who have had to go through puberty has made me passionate about teaching young girls about relationships and sex. These topics can be difficult for many families to discuss openly and honestly. Often leading to misleading conversations about what a child's peers are doing and saying. The prominence of the internet and the easy access many people (especially young children) have to it can be dangerous because not all the information available is coming from trustworthy or accurate sources.

My goal is to teach you what puberty looks like, what's normal, and when you should seek the advice of your parents or caregivers. I will discuss the hormonal changes you will undergo and how these could affect your body so you can learn how to manage and cope with these changes, including what products are available to you and which ones are recommended for use. Although, you will also have the last say as the products you are comfortable using and can afford will differ to the products other girls and women may feel comfortable using. That's completely normal and okay!

Learning about the impact of puberty on your body and emotional well-being is only the first part of understanding what's happening to you. You will also learn the difference between healthy and unhealthy relationships and sexual behaviors, including unwanted pregnancies, sexually transmitted diseases (STIs), and the truth about consensual sex. This includes understanding the different laws in the United States regarding the sexual activities for minors, your rights, what sexual grooming looks like, and the dangers of online predators. You will also learn about the importance of taking care of your mental and emotional well-being as you go through puberty and face its host of challenges.

We live in a world where the expectations placed upon women—specifically young girls—by men and society make it easy for young girls to be taken advantage of. Learning accurate information about what is happening to your body as you go through puberty, how to keep yourself healthy and safe, as well as your rights, are all important aspects of sex education that can help you keep yourself safe and build healthy relationships.

Education also prevents others from taking advantage of you and your inexperience. While talking about relationships and sex can be extremely awkward and uncomfortable, the knowledge you gain gives you the opportunity to empower yourself and successfully deal with the challenges and pressures you will face as a teenage girl. Chapter 1 will provide you with the foundation you need for your journey to better understand how puberty could affect you.

NOTES TO SELF

Write your thoughts, feelings, comments and anything you need to get off your chest or just make notes. This is your book, your space, take control.

NOTES TO SELF

Write your thoughts, feelings, comments and anything you need to get off your chest or just make notes. This is your book, your space, take control.

Chapter 1:

Let's Talk About You

Happiness and confidence are the prettiest things you can wear. –
Taylor Swift

Teenagers are often stereotyped as being moody and isolated. However, it's quite understandable when you think about it. You are at a stage in your life when your hormones are rapidly fluctuating and you're starting to experience emotions you've never felt before. On top of that, you're becoming more independent and taking on more responsibility at home and at school. You're also learning who you are as a person, and she can be different to who you were when you were younger. It's normal for a person to grow and evolve as an individual when they learn new things about themselves and the world. But it can also be stressful, especially when you're worried your parents might not accept who you really are.

While your parents were once where you are now, they may still struggle to understand why you seem to be changing who you are every week because they still see you as their baby who would wave at strangers and feel curious about the mundane. Puberty and adolescence are hard for you and your caregivers, but that doesn't mean you can't find happiness and enjoy your teenage years.

Finding Happiness

Happiness looks different for everyone. You may find that your friends, family, and even your pets make you smile and laugh, but at the end of the day, your happiness comes from within you. You also can't be happy all the time. Allowing yourself to feel and express other emotions like sadness, anger, excitement, etc. are all important for helping you stay emotionally healthy. However, you may find that the changes you experience during puberty (like changes in your hormone levels at different times of the month) can sometimes make it difficult to embrace the things that normally make you happy.

Fortunately, there are a few common ways for you to introduce happiness in your daily life. One of the main strategies is to ensure you are satisfied with your life and relationships. You could also praise yourself for things, no matter how small they are. Perhaps you hate doing the dishes but they're part of your chores. You could set a timer and try to finish washing the dishes before the timer goes off. Every time you succeed, praise yourself. This applies to almost anything you have to do during the day. The aim of activities like this is to show yourself appreciation and acknowledge your hard work. This may seem a bit odd, but giving yourself the attention and encouragement you crave, without having to rely on others can help you learn to value your own strengths. Even if you make a mistake, you should be proud of yourself for trying anyway. Being proud of who you are, even if that person doesn't fit into the mold created by others, is important for finding happiness within yourself.

Accepting Your Body

How you see and feel about your body, as well as how you think your body looks compared to how it looks in reality, is known as your "body image" (*Body image: Pre-teens and teenagers*, 2022: par. 7). You may find it hard to accept your body when society and the media are constantly pushing unrealistic body standards on girls from a young age. This is even more difficult when your body doesn't fit into the so-called "ideal body type." But in reality, no woman can safely and realistically achieve the body standards pushed on us by society. The bodies you see in the media have often been photoshopped to look that way, but that doesn't mean your body is any less deserving of love, care, and appreciation.

You also need to remember that your genetics play a role in how your body will change shape as you grow up; however, you will mainly notice these changes during puberty. That's why taking care of your body and showing it the love and appreciation it deserves is so important. As you grow up, the way you see and feel about your body will change. Your environment, social media, friends, peers, family members, and cultural background are just some of the factors that could influence your body image as you grow up. But you may find it hard to appreciate your body during adolescence because the changes you are undergoing can be quite noticeable during a time when you might not want to be noticed or stand out.

A negative body image can be triggered by seemingly harmless or subtle comments about your body, weight, or size. Society has normalized commenting on young girls' bodies, but that doesn't mean it's okay or won't hurt you. You may not even be aware of these comments until you find yourself refusing to wear certain clothes or eat specific foods, but diets are not the answer to improving your body image. They can actually have a really harmful impact on your mental, emotional, and physical health that could affect you for many years to come. So how do you improve the way you see yourself?

You could start out by appreciating your body for what it can do and not for how it looks. Acknowledging and praising your body for giving you the energy to get through your day or the strength to help your friend decorate their bedroom are simple examples of appreciating your body for its abilities and not its looks. It's easy for others to criticize women for not having a flat stomach, but they forget that your genetics play an important role in determining your body size and shape. Girls also have an extra organ (your uterus) that can press against your abdomen, especially during your period, causing you to have a small pouch. Your body also goes through different phases during your cycle where it changes size and shape. Humans also have a layer of fat that keeps your organs safe. This layer just happens to look different on different body types and that's perfectly okay. However, you need to be able to recognize the warning signs of a negative body image.

Warning Signs of a Negative Body Image

There are a number of different warning signs of a negative body image. You may find that you've already experienced some of these warning signs. Or you may have experienced signs not included here. Everyone is affected by the media, negative opinions, and pressure differently. Create your own list of warning signs to help you identify or notice when the way you see yourself is not as positive as it used to be. Use the list of warning signs that follows as a starting point.

- Wearing baggy or loose clothing for reasons other than comfort, or wearing clothes you don't actually like so you can hide your body.

- Feeling guilty or ashamed when you eat, especially when eating foods like pasta, bread, chocolate, cookies, etc.

- Obsessing over your weight or the way specific body parts look (like your arms, stomach, legs, or face).

- Taking pictures so you can scrutinize them for possible flaws or imperfections so you can try and fix them.

- Feeling like you need cosmetic procedures to fix these "imperfections."

- Changing your eating habits to gain more control over your weight.

- Exercising for reasons other than improving your mental and physical health.

A person's weight and size cannot always be equated to their health. A negative body image can lower your self-esteem and put you at risk of developing eating disorders and mental disorders like depression and anxiety. If you feel that the way you view your body is interfering with your ability to go about your daily life or appreciate yourself, please ask your parents, caregivers, or school counselors to help you seek the assistance of a qualified medical professional.

Reflective Activity

Using the information discussed here as a starting point, I want you to make a list of the things you appreciate about your body, including what your body does for you, to help you appreciate your body as you go about your day. When you notice the warning signs of a negative body image, you can use this list to show your body appreciation and help you feel more positive toward yourself.

Coping With Your Moods

Fluctuating moods are quite normal, especially when you're going through puberty. This doesn't mean these fluctuations aren't frustrating or confusing though. There are a number of reasons why your mood is constantly shifting. As you enter puberty, you begin to develop sex hormones that have the ability to trigger physical changes and sexual and romantic feelings. These emotions are more mature than you are used to and can be confusing at first. You also become more independent during this stage of your life, so you have to learn how to solve problems on your own.

Managing strong emotions, new thoughts, and responsibilities, and facing the challenges of adolescence can be quite stressful. Luckily, you can learn how to manage these changes and new emotions in a way that helps you cope with them in a healthy manner.

Tips for Boosting Your Mood

Taking part in activities or hobbies that help you feel at peace or happy is a great way to process new emotions and prepare yourself to face challenges. Hobbies like painting, music, poetry, meditation, or yoga are some activities that can help you cope with challenging emotions. However, there are four main ways you can improve your ability to cope with these changes and boost your mood as you move through adolescence.

- **Emotional intelligence:** Your ability to identify, understand, evaluate, control, and use your emotions to effectively communicate and relate to others in a healthy way is known as "emotional intelligence" (Cherry, 2022b: par. 3). This skill can help you actively listen to others so you can better understand how they are feeling and see things from their point of view. This skill is useful for developing your ability to empathize with others so you can understand why they are behaving in a certain way. Emotional intelligence is also useful for helping you understand how your emotions can affect your decisions and behaviors in different situations.

- **Resilience:** Building your capacity for resilience can help you handle the pressure of being an adolescent *and* improve your ability to face challenges and cope in a healthy way. Finding your purpose for this stage in your life—by volunteering at an animal shelter, learning a new skill, or focusing on yourself—and making new friends, staying optimistic and positive about life, developing your problem-solving skills, embracing change, acting on your goals, and believing in yourself and your abilities are some examples which can help you develop your resilience.

- **Self-compassion:** Showing yourself forgiveness, accepting who you are right now, and loving yourself despite your circumstances are some ways you can show yourself compassion. Essentially, you would treat yourself like you would your best friend. Positive affirmations are a great tool to help you show yourself appreciation throughout the day.

- **Confidence:** Being confident is difficult during puberty, but you can improve your confidence by acknowledging accomplishments that feed your passion and make you feel happy and proud of who you are. Use your goals to help you get things done and monitor your progress as you move through adolescence. Goals don't have to be life-changing; even small goals are important. Doing the right thing, even if no one else is, can help you define who you are as a person. Embracing your mistakes and not allowing a fear of failure to hold you back can create learning opportunities that help you become the person you truly are. Believing in yourself and following through with what you say can increase your self-respect and make it easier to overcome challenges in the future. It doesn't matter what other people think. If you are happy with who you are and how you are living your life, then it's with all the effort and hard work you are putting in.

Looking After Your Mental Health

As a growing teen, it's vital that you take care of your mental health. As you get older, your mental health may change, and go through different stages of highs and lows. It's quite normal for girls because your hormone levels fluctuate throughout the month, especially when you first start your period. Being able to recognize when your mental health is declining can help you get the assistance you need to cope.

Adolescence itself can be quite a challenging time of your life, but it's also when you are at a higher risk of developing mental health problems due to the various changes your mind and body go through during such a short period. Learning to take care of your social, emotional, and psychological well-being can help you improve your mental health and manage it effectively when you do face challenges. This allows you to feel happier about who you are and can improve your ability to cope with failure, develop healthy relationships, take care of your physical health, and feel confident about your skills.

Signs of Declining Mental Health

Various signs of declining mental health exist. The warning signs you experience could differ compared to the symptoms experienced by others. You could use the list in this section to help you create your own list of warning signs so you can recognize when your mental health may be declining as early as possible. This allows you to seek the help you need to manage your mental health. If your experience of the symptoms discussed below lasts longer than two weeks or interferes with your daily life, please ask your parents, caregivers, or school counselors to help you seek the assistance of a qualified mental health professional:

- You don't want to be around other people, including your friends and family members.

- It's difficult for you to fall or stay asleep.

- You feel anxious about your physical appearance.

- Physical pain such as stomachache, headache, or backache that doesn't want to go away.

- Difficulties focusing in school or you are more forgetful than usual.

- Sudden changes in your behavior and mood that you can't explain.

- A loss of appetite.

- Difficulties coping with regular daily activities that you never struggled with before.

- You feel hopeless, lack motivation, or feel sad.

How to Talk to Others About Your Mental Well-Being

You may find it hard to talk to others about your mental health. It's understandable as mental health can be incredibly personal, but mental health issues that are left untreated can have a significant negative impact on your physical health, relationships, development, and well-being. You could make a list of the people in your life that you trust or feel comfortable talking to, including family members, friends, school counselors, your healthcare provider, an elder, religious leader, sports coach, or community leader.

Sharing your thoughts and feelings with someone you trust can help you gain a new perspective on a situation and provide you with the guidance and support you need to cope with these emotions. You are not alone. Many people, regardless of their age, struggle with their mental health. The key is learning how to take care of your mental health as you face the challenges created by adolescence.

When to Ask Your Parents or Guardians to Take You to a Doctor

When you notice your mental health begins to significantly interfere with your daily life, you should ask your parents or guardians to help you seek the assistance of a qualified mental health provider such as a psychologist, local community healthcare center, counselor, or your local state or territory mental health services. While opening up about your mental health struggles can be daunting, it can help you receive the love and support you need to cope with the challenges of adolescence and puberty. The support and guidance of family and friends can play a vital role in helping you better understand your needs so you can grow up into a confident and independent young woman.

Learning to take care of yourself and embrace the changes you are going through can help you build a solid foundation for ensuring you keep yourself safe and healthy as you move through adolescence and puberty. It isn't easy, but the work you put in to take care of yourself is worth it. Learning to take care of yourself as an individual also means learning about the physical changes you will go through as you reach puberty. Chapter 2 will help you better understand how puberty might affect your body.

NOTES TO SELF

Write your thoughts, feelings, comments and anything you need to get off your chest or just make notes. This is your book, your space, take control.

NOTES TO SELF

Write your thoughts, feelings, comments and anything you need to get off your chest or just make notes. This is your book, your space, take control.

Chapter 2:

Let's Talk About Your Body

I was the ugly duckling until I reached puberty. –Tanya Roberts

Puberty can seem like one of the scariest stages of your life. You may even have already learned some things about puberty from school, the adults in your life, your peers, or the internet. Regardless of what you have learned, you may feel overwhelmed by the drastic changes you will face during your adolescent years and as much as you might want to avoid it, you can't stop a biological process. But that doesn't mean you can't survive puberty and enjoy your teenage years. Sure, puberty can make life more challenging, but learning what to expect can help you prepare for and face these changes head-on.

While I will provide you with an easy-to-understand explanation about what physical changes you can expect, you may still have questions. That's great! The best way to learn is to ask questions, even if you feel awkward asking them. To lessen some of the anxiety you might feel, you can create a list of questions as you work through this book. These questions will most likely be answered in later chapters as everything has been broken down into smaller sections to prevent you from becoming overwhelmed, but if you have a question that isn't answered here, you could ask your parents, caregivers, or family members for help. A trusted healthcare provider also has the ability to answer questions related to your developing body.

As awkward and embarrassing as it may feel to discuss puberty with the people you trust, gaining knowledge gives you the power to keep yourself safe and help you improve and maintain your health as you get older. You can start your journey to better understand what happens to your body by learning about the five stages of puberty.

Five Stages of Puberty

I keep talking about puberty, but you may be wondering what it actually is. Puberty is a specific period in your life when you will undergo physical, mental, and emotional changes that allow you to make the transition from child to adult. This stage can be quite awkward as your body develops and changes to become sexually mature, preparing your body for future reproduction. Puberty may begin at different ages for different girls, but it generally begins between the ages

Changes in Your Body

While the five stages of puberty give you some insight into what will happen to your body, I will discuss these changes in slightly more detail so you can better understand why these changes occur and how they can affect you during your adolescence. Let's start with the brain so you can better understand how puberty is triggered.

Brain

Puberty is triggered when a chemical called the "gonadotropin-releasing hormone (GnRH)" is released by your brain. This hormone will travel to your pituitary gland (a pea-shaped gland found underneath your brain) which will release two additional hormones into your bloodstream. The luteinizing hormone (LH) and the follicle-stimulating hormone (FSH) can be found in both girls' and boys' bodies, but they work on different parts of the body. In girls, the ovaries (which contain your eggs) are targeted by the LH and FSH hormones.

Estrogen (another hormone found in higher levels in girls than boys), FSH, and LH are all responsible for preparing your body for maturity, specifically sexual maturity. In other words, these chemicals are released in your body to prepare you to go from a teenager to an adult with adult hormone levels. Girls generally begin puberty between the ages of 7 and 13; however, some girls may start earlier or later.

Height

As you enter puberty, you will notice that your body begins to grow faster than you might expect. This is normal. Even your height will increase. This period of increased growth is commonly called a "growth spurt." You could grow up to four inches or more in one year, for two to three years; however, your height will depend on a number of factors, including genetics, your environment, and nutrition, to name a few. Some girls may find they stop growing at about 16 years old, while others may continue to grow. Once this growth spurt is over, you will have reached your adult height.

Weight

Weight can be a very sensitive subject, especially as society expects women to stay the same weight for their entire life. They also place our worth and beauty on our weight. This has created a number of issues for girls, including problems with confidence, self-esteem, body image, and eating disorders.

The truth is, your weight will constantly change throughout your life. These fluctuations might not be very noticeable, but you should not place your worth or self-esteem on your weight. Puberty causes you to gain weight and can change your body shape. You will find that your hips begin to widen, your breasts grow, and you may notice an increase in body fat. All girls experience this.

Don't allow others to pressure you into dieting or exercising solely to lose weight. Weight gain during puberty is healthy and natural. Your body is going through a number of changes that trigger this increase in weight. However, if you are concerned about your weight—especially significant unexplained weight gain or loss—you should speak with your healthcare provider to ensure there are no underlying issues or health problems.

Acne

Unfortunately, as your hormone levels fluctuate during puberty, you may find that your skin is oilier than usual. This can trigger acne. The type of acne you experience, including its severity, will differ from your peers and can depend on a number of factors. If you are concerned about your acne—especially if it's severe— speak with your healthcare provider.

In general, you should keep your skin clean by using a face wash that suits your skin type. For example, if you have very oily skin, you can buy a face wash that states it's suitable for oily skin on its label. After washing your face (don't scrub your skin, be gentle) you can pat it dry with a soft, clean towel and then use a moisturizer designed for the face (not all skincare products can be used on your face so be sure to check their labels). Washing your face in the mornings and in the evenings will be important and you should put sunscreen on after your moisturizer in the mornings to protect your skin.

The types of products you use and the skincare routine that suits your needs will differ to your peers. Some girls have complex skin routines that involve additional serums and moisturizers, while other girls keep their routines simple because their skin is sensitive and requires special products.

Skin problems and allergies can play an important role in the types of products you use, so you may need to seek the guidance of your healthcare provider. Healthcare providers can also recommend suitable products and routines if you do have sensitive skin or allergies.

Sore and Growing Breasts

I briefly discussed this during the five stages of puberty. It's normal for your nipples to become sore as your breasts begin to grow. The development of your breast buds is your earliest sign that you've entered puberty.

This bump may develop on one breast before the other, but your other breast will catch up. Fortunately, the tenderness and soreness of your breasts should improve over time. As in the previous sections, if the pain is severe, seek the assistance of your healthcare provider. During this time, you may also begin looking at buying bras. There are a variety of bras available. With the development of your breast buds, training bras are a good start due to their soft, comfortable material.

I would recommend asking a female figure in your life that you trust to help you buy your first bra. Clothing stores that sell bras—especially lingerie stores—have specialists that can help you correctly fit your bra. You have to remember that as your breasts grow, your bra size will change too. Generally, a well-fitted bra should not cause pain in your back and shoulders, restrict your breathing or movement, or cause you discomfort. Fitting your own bra can be quite challenging when you don't know what to look for, but you can use the following tips to help you size yourself correctly.

1. Using a measuring tape, measure around your ribcage, just under your breasts. Take this measurement and add four to five inches to find your band size.

2. Measure around the widest part of your bare bust (the point of your breasts where your nipple can be found) while keeping the measuring tape as level as possible. Compare

your bust size to your band size to find a starting size of bras to try on. For example, if your bust size is up to half an inch larger than your band size, your cup size is AA, half to one inch larger is A, one to two inches larger is a B, two to three inches bigger is a C, three to four inches is a D, and four to five inches is a DD or an E cup (*How to find the right bra*, 2015:par. 13-20)

At the store, you can try on various styles of bras to find what you are most comfortable with. In the changing room, adjust the straps to sit comfortably on your shoulders, and then use the tips below to determine whether the bra fits correctly or not.

- The band of the bra should be comfortable, without digging into your skin or ribcage, it should sit level and not ride up your back, and it should not allow the cups of the bra to let your breasts slip out.

- Correctly fitting cups are filled by your breasts without them overflowing. You can bend forward to ensure your breasts don't slip out and the cup's fabric should not wrinkle.

- The fabric of the cups should lie flat against your breast bone and you should be able to lift and move your arms without the cups moving or sliding off your breasts.

- Your nipples should be centered to the fullest part of the cup.

After finding and buying bras that fit you, take note of their tags that indicate how to take care of them. Bras that are not well-cared for can stretch out and fit incorrectly after only a few washes.

Body Hair

Your body hair will grow, increase in thickness, and become darker during puberty. You will notice hair beginning to grow under your arms and on and around your genitals. It will start out thin and light before becoming thicker, darker, and longer. This is normal but this growth may also make you feel uncomfortable or self-conscious.

There are no medical reasons for shaving armpit or leg hair—unless you are undergoing surgery—but if you feel self-conscious about this hair or would like to remove it, you could use methods such as shaving or waxing (Allen and Miller, 2019: par. 7).

Body hair is natural and as long as you are showering or bathing regularly, this hair is clean. While it's nice to have smooth legs, it does take continuous effort to keep up with shaving and waxing. So if you do decide to remove this hair but have a few days where your leg hair is a bit longer than normal, don't feel bad about it.

Body Odor

Entering puberty also means gaining a few new smells, including body odor. Body odor is normal, and everyone gets it. Puberty hormones affect your skin glands, causing them to emit chemicals that smell bad. Showering or bathing daily, as well as using deodorants or antiperspirants, can help you decrease the severity of this smell as you go about your day.

Vaginal Discharge

As your hormones begin to increase and you approach menstruation, you will notice discharge in your underwear. Discharge is a white or clear mucus-like substance that comes from your vagina. It will change in color, smell, and consistency throughout your menstruation cycle as it indicates changes in your hormones. When you notice discharge in your underwear, you can use pantyliners (discussed in the next section) to improve your comfort. This is also a sign to ensure you maintain your hygiene. You can use the following tips to help you stay clean and feel more comfortable as you go about your day.

- When you take your daily shower or bath, ensure you gently wash your intimate areas, especially if you are exercising or swimming. Some women use an intimate wash, but it isn't necessary. The vagina is a self-cleaning organ (which is why an intimate wash isn't necessary) so a gentle wash using an unscented soap to clean the external genital area—especially your pubic hair—is more than appropriate (Villines, 2020: par. 1).

- Once washed, ensure you thoroughly rinse off all the soap or product from your intimate areas.

- Dry off thoroughly with a clean towel. Infections normally occur when there is a build-up of moisture. This is why when you do use pantyliners, pads, or tampons, you should change them regularly to ensure the health of your intimate areas.

Periods

Every girl's period cycle will be different. Stress, environmental factors, genetics, underlying health issues, etc., are just some of the factors that can impact your period's cycle. When you first start menstruating, your cycle will also be very irregular. Keeping pads, tampons, and pantyliners in your bag or on your person even before starting your period can help you stay prepared should your period begin unexpectedly. Unfortunately, periods can be quite unpredictable when you are a teen. Girls generally start their period around

12 years old and your cycle can range between 21 to 35 days.

You may begin to feel bloated, eat more, experience muscle and joint pain, feel tired, or have a lower mood or increased anxiety during the days leading up to your period. Some girls also experience cramping before their period starts. You can take pain medication like ibuprofen to help manage this pain. A hot water bottle placed on your abdomen can also help with cramping. However, if your cramps are so severe you cannot move or go to school, you need to see your healthcare provider as there may be an underlying issue.

In general, every period is based on the following information: You have two ovaries that hold thousands of eggs that have been there since you were born. When you enter puberty and begin your menstrual cycle, one egg will come out of one of your ovaries and travel down your fallopian tube (the tube connecting the ovary to the uterus, also called the "womb") into your uterus. However, before the egg was released, your uterus was building up its lining using blood and tissue to make a comfortable environment for the egg.

If an egg is fertilized by a sperm cell, the egg cell will stay in the uterus and grow into a baby using this blood and tissue to develop. When there is no sperm cell to fertilize this egg, the egg passes through. Your uterus no longer needs this extra blood and tissue, so your period is the result of your uterus getting rid of this lining through your vagina. This causes your menstrual period and could last between five to seven days. About two weeks after the start of your period, a new egg will be released from your ovaries, marking the middle of your menstrual cycle (*Everything you wanted to know about puberty*, n.d.: par. 19-21).

This is a very simplified explanation of your period, but I want you to understand why you have a period and what the blood leaving your body is. You can use the next section to help you decide what products you would like to use during your period. In general, you should ensure that you stay as hygienic as possible during your period to keep yourself healthy as old blood can cause problems for your continued health.

Products for Your Vanity Cabinet

There are a multitude of products aimed at women available at your local drug store and grocery store. The products you use will depend on what you can afford, what you are comfortable using, as well as any skin issues or other allergies you might have. This section will provide you with a broad overview of the different products you should keep in your vanity cabinet.

Skincare products

The best skincare products are the ones suited to your skin type. If you have allergies or sensitive skin, you may need to ask your healthcare provider for product recommendations. A basic skincare routine consists of a cleanser, toner, and moisturizer. Each product will have directions that can guide you on how to use them correctly and when. Some girls may use additional products, like a hydrating serum or spot treatment, to cater to their skin's unique needs. You can start with a basic skincare routine and then decide whether you should use additional products or not.

Sunscreen

You should put on sunscreen every morning after completing your skincare routine. Sunscreen can decrease your risk of developing different skin cancers and precancers. There are various sunscreens available, but the protection your sunscreen offers should be effective and broad. SPF 15 or higher is recommended by the Skin Cancer Foundation (*All about sunscreen*, 2022: par. 24).

Razors, Shaving Cream, or Wax

Removing your body hair is a personal choice and no other person has a say in it. Regardless of what you choose, you should know which products are available and how you can use them. Razors, shaving cream, and wax can be bought from your drugstore or grocery store.

There are a number of products available but you should check the packaging for products labeled for women. Before shaving, an adult (your mother or female caregiver) should show you how to use a razor correctly so you can avoid irritating your skin or accidentally cutting it. This can cause a skin infection or other skin issues.

If you decide to shave, you will first need to wet your skin. Shaving while in the bath or shower may be best as a result. Use your soap, lotion, or gel to create a protective layer on your skin to avoid cuts and irritation. Take your razor and, using a gentle yet light pressure, begin shaving your legs in slow strokes.

Ensure you thoroughly rinse your razor in warm water to clean the blade. You will find that the skin around your ankles and knees may be more sensitive than the rest of your skin, so remember to be gentle. Shaving takes practice, but as long as you are careful you will be okay. After shaving, rinse the skin thoroughly and dry off with a clean towel. You can then use a body cream to moisturize your legs. Ensure you never share razors and that you replace your razor often to avoid using a dull or rusted blade. This can expose you to bacteria.

Oils for Stretch Marks

Stretch marks are natural and do fade over time; however, some girls aren't comfortable with them. That's okay, you are already going through a very challenging time in your life. You can use various oils to help your stretch marks fade quicker. According to Leonard (2018), the following essential oils can be used to help your stretch marks fade:

- bitter almond oil

- argan oil

- lavender oil

- bitter orange oil

- patchouli oil

- neroli oil

- pomegranate oil

- frankincense oil

Warning: Do not ingest these oils or apply them directly onto your skin! Essential oils can burn and irritate your skin when directly applied. I would recommend carefully reading the labels of oils specifically designed for reducing stretch marks and purchasing the stretch mark serums containing the essential oils mentioned above.

Pantyliners

Pantyliners are thin, absorbent pads and can protect your underwear from discharge and the spotting which occurs at the end of your period (*What are pantyliners for? Are they good for you?* 2023:par.2). You should change your panty liner every three to four hours to prevent a buildup of moisture. It also keeps you feeling fresh and clean.

Tampons and Pads

Tampons, pads, and menstrual cups are used to soak up menstrual blood. The product you decide to use will depend on what you can afford, what you are comfortable using, and what feels right. As with the other products you should keep in your vanity cabinet, there are a number of menstrual products and brands to choose from. (*Tampons, pads, and other period supplies*, 2019)

Pads

Pads are attached inside your underwear, similar to pantyliners except they have wings, to soak up your period blood. Also known as sanitary pads or napkins, the wings fold over the side of your underwear to hold the pad in place and prevent leaks (*Tampons, pads, and other period supplies*, 2019: par. 7). The type of pad you use (super, mini, slender, maxi, or overnight) will depend on the amount you bleed during your period. You may even have days where your flow is lighter or heavier than on other days.

When buying pads, choose one that will be large enough to prevent leaks, but small enough for you to feel comfortable. Pads should be changed every three to four hours for a light flow, but may need more regular changing if your flow is heavier.

Tampons

A tube-shaped absorbent material that absorbs your menstrual blood from inside your vagina (*Tampons, pads, and other period supplies*, 2019: par. 24). They come in different sizes and absorbencies depending on your flow. Just like pads, tampons need regular changing. Change your tampon every four to six hours by gently pulling on the string that remains outside the vagina after inserting the tampon. Wrap it in toilet paper and throw it in the trash.

The way tampons are inserted into your vagina will depend on the type of tampon you bought. If you wash your hands, relax, and follow the instructions, you will be okay.

Please note: You should **never** leave a tampon in all day or all night (regardless of your flow) as you can put yourself at risk of a dangerous disease called "toxic shock syndrome" (*Tampons, pads, and other period supplies*, 2019: par. 36).

Menstrual Cup

Similar to a tampon, a menstrual cup is inserted into your vagina, but it catches the blood instead of absorbing it. As such they are normally made from a special rubber or silicone so you can use them again. Menstrual cups come with instructions for use and care instructions. You will need to ensure that you take proper care of your menstrual cup to prevent bacteria from making you ill.

While the period products you use will depend on your preference, some girls also switch between each product depending on their daily schedule. Choose the product you are comfortable with and feel confident using. You may even find that you start out with pads but would like to alternate with tampons as you move through adolescence. Either way, keep a few period products on your person or in your bag even when you aren't on your period as periods are irregular when you first begin to menstruate.

Your body goes through a number of changes at a fast rate when you enter adolescence. It's easy to become overwhelmed, but you will be okay! Many women have been where you are, and your peers are going through the same thing too. Take a breath, read this chapter again, and start thinking about how **you** want to approach your first period. Your lifestyle also changes as you go through puberty. Chapter 3 will help you understand what these changes are, what you can expect, and how you can educate yourself so you can stay safe.

NOTES TO SELF

Write your thoughts, feelings, comments and anything you need to get off your chest or just make notes. This is your book, your space, take control.

NOTES TO SELF

Write your thoughts, feelings, comments and anything you need to get off your chest or just make notes. This is your book, your space, take control.

Chapter 3:

Let's Talk About Your

Lifestyle

I never dreamed about success. I worked for it. –Estée Lauder

Your entire life changes as you go through adolescence. This change is accompanied by a number of challenges that can influence the direction of your life. John C. Maxwell, an American motivational speaker, once said that, "Change is inevitable, growth is optional" and it's true, especially as a teenager (*"Change is inevitable, growth is optional quote*," 2021: par. 33-34). While you can't control how puberty will affect you or your life, you can choose what to do about these changes and how to make them work for you. However, being able to take control of these changes doesn't mean it's easy to do so. Fortunately, there are a number of tips you can use to improve your lifestyle.

Create Healthy Habits

The media, society, your teachers, mentors, and parents are probably always telling you to make the right choice and live a healthy life, especially as you enter adolescence. However, everyone's idea of a healthy habit is different. For society and the media, healthy habits for women often center around looking our best and living up to their expectations of how a woman should be living her life, but that doesn't mean these expectations are right for you or even healthy. Everyone has different needs that change throughout their life. It's up to you to find out what works best and how you want to live your life.

While society and the media may have unrealistic expectations of teenage girls, researchers have put in the work to create some useful guidelines for creating basic healthy habits. One key tip to creating successful healthy habits is to break these habits up into smaller, more manageable tasks. You might find yourself becoming overwhelmed if you try to implement a number of new habits at the same time. Instead, you could start by introducing a single healthy habit at a time using the core habits discussed in the section that follows.

Sleep

Sleep is very important for your mental and physical health. As a teenager, you may find it easy to sleep for longer periods because your body is exhausted after a day of coping with the changes puberty brings. Try to aim for between 8 to 10 hours of sleep every night. If you struggle to fall asleep, try to avoid screen time for 15 to 30 minutes before bed. You could also create a nightly routine that involves steps like changing into your pajamas, doing your skincare routine, and brushing your teeth. Having a set routine can help your mind shutdown, and prepare for bed.

Diet

It can be difficult to eat healthy when you don't have as much control over your diet as an adult with a job would. Healthier food options can also be expensive depending on where you live. When you can, try to choose healthy food options. For example, you could swap out a cup of coffee in the evening with a cup of tea, or you could change your study snacks of cookies and gummies to healthier options like an apple that's been cut into smaller pieces. This doesn't mean you can never have takeout or eat sweets. The key is *moderation* because even too much of a healthy food can be bad, like eating too many carrots can turn your skin orange even though carrots are healthy (Family Health Team, 2019: par. 1-3).

Exercise

Exercise is important too, but it isn't always about losing weight or building muscle. Exercise increases your circulation and the amount of oxygen in your body, which is good for your mental and physical health. That's why mental health experts may advise you to go for a 20-minute walk if you are struggling with mental health issues like depression. In general, you should be getting 30 to 60 minutes of physical exercise every day (*Happiness and wellbeing for pre-teens and teenagers*, 2022: par. 23).

You could break this time up into two separate sessions during the day, or even several 10-minute sessions throughout your day. It may take a bit of experimentation, but find out what works for you. The key to creating an exercise habit is to do an activity that you enjoy. If you can go outside, try going for a brisk walk around the block or swimming at school, your local community center, or at the gym. Cycling, running, and hiking are a few additional outdoor activities you could try too.

However, if you can't go outside or don't feel comfortable exercising outside, you could exercise at home. Yoga, Pilates, and other at-home exercise routines are available online. *YouTube* has a number of different channels you could make use of. Search the name of the exercise you are looking for—like hip hop for beginners or yoga for beginners—and first watch a few different videos before deciding which one you are comfortable using. Then, you could clear a space in your bedroom to practice these exercises.

Some people will clear out enough space to lie down on their bedroom floor without knocking anything over. They then use their bed or desk chair to help with exercises like sit-ups or tricep dips.

The way you organize your bedroom will depend on the activity you are doing. Yoga could be done on a bedroom rug, while practicing hip-hop may need a bit more space. You should ensure you can't knock anything off your desk, shelves, or bedside table when dancing.

Once you have successfully introduced these habits into your life, you can begin building additional habits like taking part in hobbies, extra-curricular activities, or working on your goals. They are also useful for catering to your mental health needs, but you have to be patient.

It will take time to build habits and stick to them. If you make mistakes or forget something, don't punish yourself. Notice your mistake, forgive yourself, reflect on why you may have forgotten this habit, and think about how you can avoid doing it again.

You learn how to solve problems and better understand why a specific habit is more challenging to build compared to another. Building a healthy routine that suits your lifestyle takes time and requires you to find the right balance. Forgiving yourself for making mistakes and being patient can help you avoid feeling overwhelmed. But creating healthy habits isn't the only key to living a healthy life.

Cigarettes, Vaping, Drugs, and Alcohol

Many of the tv series aimed at teens frame adolescence and high school as a time of your life when you will drink alcohol, try drugs, party, or have sex. While this may be true for some teenagers, it isn't a universal experience. You don't need to take part in these activities to enjoy your adolescence. However, there are a number of reasons why many teenagers decide to experiment with drugs or alcohol.

Peer Pressure

Peer pressure is one of the main reasons for experimenting with drugs, cigarettes, and alcohol. After all, you don't want to feel left out, but that doesn't mean these activities are safe. These substances are also readily available and consumed by the people in your life. When something seems so normal, it's hard to think of it as being wrong.

Media Influences

Many TV series, movies, and adverts aimed at teens have normalized the use of drugs, smoking, and alcohol. They also make these substances appear safe to use so it becomes easy to ignore your parents and teachers' constant warnings about the dangers of such substances. But just because it appears to be cool and safe in a fictional world doesn't mean it's safe in reality.

Escape From Problems

Your teen years are accompanied by a number of new emotions of varying intensities thanks to fluctuating hormone levels. This can make even regular emotions difficult to cope with. For some girls, emotions like anxiety, sadness, and general unhappiness with the changes they are experiencing can become very difficult to cope with. They may feel like turning to substances, like drugs and alcohol, are the only way to cope. Drugs, alcohol, and cigarettes are made up of chemicals that interact with your nervous system to provide you with altered versions of happiness, contentment, focus, and energy, but they can also cause irreparable damage to your mind, body, and life.

Self-Medicating

Prescription medications are easy to access in your home and some teens use them to help them cope with intense emotions. These substances are often used to cope with things like social, academic, and emotional stressors which become more intense as you grow up.

Boredom

Boredom can be physically and emotionally painful for some individuals, especially if you struggle to keep yourself occupied or crave excitement and adrenaline. The way substances, like alcohol and drugs, interact with your nervous system can imitate emotions and may act as a bonding tool among your friend group, regardless of whether it's safe or not.

Rebellion

Many parents and teachers believe rebellion is the main reason for teens using these substances, but as you learned from the rest of this section, that isn't always true. However, when teenagers use a substance to rebel, alcohol is often used by teens who feel angry; escape drugs, like LSD, are hallucinogens that allow teens to escape to a more accepting and idealistic world, and cigarettes are used by teens trying to show their independence to their parents. But these are only some of the possible reasons why a teenager might use a substance.

Instant Gratification

Drugs and alcohol don't make you wait to feel satisfied, happy, relaxed, or energized. This makes them appealing to teens who want to feel instantly happy without having to wait.

Lack of Confidence

Drugs and alcohol can help you fake confidence because of the way they interact with your brain and nervous system. They do this by taking away your inhibitions and alleviating social anxiety, two factors that often hold teenagers back if they are self-conscious or lack confidence.

Misinformation

A lot of inaccurate information about drugs, alcohol, and smoking exists. Especially due to the way the media portrays the use of such substances in series and movies. I would not recommend using any of the substances discussed in this chapter, but if you ever decide that you want to experiment with a substance like alcohol or weed, it's critical that you do your own research. This doesn't mean asking your friend who is a supposed "expert" on the substance. Speak with researchers or go online and look up information on credible websites like *Mayo Clinic*, the *Centers for Disease Control and Prevention*, and addiction centers.

No one can stop you from being curious about these substances or even experimenting with them, but you have the responsibility to do your own research about how these substances could affect you, as well as the risks of using them. Entering adolescence means you are transitioning into an adult and learning to take responsibility is a part of that.

The Dangers of Using Legal and Illegal Substances

You're probably wondering why substances that are commonly used by people in your life, celebrities, friends, and in the media are so dangerous. The way cigarettes, vaping, drugs, and alcohol affect a person will be unique, but there are a number of potential health risks that accompany the use of these substances.

Cigarette Smoking

There are a number of common dangers associated with cigarette smoking, including:

- reduced lung growth and functioning

- nicotine addiction

- early heart damage

- an impact on brain development

- decreased stamina

- shortness of breath (CDC, 2014: par. 8)

Vaping

Vaping has become a popular alternative to smoking because it's believed that vaping is safer. However, the poor regulation of vaping devices and the chemicals used to make vape juice means there is a possibility vaping can have as many negative effects as smoking regular cigarettes can (Barghouty, 2019: par. 2 and 15). Current research has also found that e-cigarettes could be harmful to your attention, ability to learn, and memory, while also increasing your risk of using and becoming addicted to other substances in the future (*E-cigarettes and teens*, 2020: par. 8).

Popular Drugs Amongst Youth

According to Mayo Clinic Staff (2022: par. 23-29), the following drugs are popular among teenagers and can put you at risk of developing a number of health issues:

- **Opioids:** Increased risk of breathing issues and death due to overdosing.

- **Cocaine:** Increased risk of stroke, heart attack, and seizures.

- **Methamphetamine:** Long-term use can increase your risk of psychotic behaviors.

- **Ecstasy:** Increased risk of heart and liver failure.

- **Marijuana:** You are put at risk of a number of health issues, namely impaired problem-solving abilities, learning problems, concentration, and memory issues. Psychosis can also occur with frequent, long-term use.

- **Inhalants:** Increased risk of damage to your kidneys, heart, liver, and lungs.

Alcohol Abuse

Alcohol can be a dangerous substance, especially when it's abused. The teenage brain, your brain, responds differently to alcohol compared to adults (Jeurgens and Hampton, 2023: par. 22). As such, alcohol can increase your risk of a number of physical, mental, and social health issues, including:

- impacted growth

- delayed puberty

- problems at school

- fighting with your peers

- unplanned, unwanted, and unprotected sexual activity

- memory problems

- alcohol poisoning

- changes in your brain development

- physical and sexual violence

- dangerous and reckless driving

- abuse of other substances

- legal problems

- increased risk of suicide, harassment, and murder (CDC, 2022: par. 14-26)

How to Avoid Peer Pressure

Choosing to take part in activities or behaviors you would not normally take part in, but do so to feel accepted and valued by your peers and friends is known as "peer pressure" (*Peer pressure or influence: Pre-teens and teenagers*, 2021: par. 7). You have probably been warned by the adults in your life to avoid doing something just because your friends are, but how do you avoid giving into peer pressure?

- **Learn to say no:** When you crave acceptance and don't want to stand out, saying "no" can be hard. However, this single word can keep you safe and healthy, and it can help you avoid putting yourself in an uncomfortable position. True friends won't ask you to explain why you are saying "no," or to apologize for saying "no." If you find it easier to decline something by providing an explanation, then keep it short, and don't be afraid to give a fake excuse, like your mom will smell smoke on you no matter what because she has an insanely good sense of smell. You may feel bad, but you will be safe and healthy and sometimes that's more important than being accepted or pressured into something dangerous by your peers.

- **Create a way out:** If you go to a party or out with friends and you're worried about being put in an unsafe situation or pressured into using a substance, you and your parents (or caregivers) could have an agreed-upon code word—like butter, bread, earache, or headache—that can be worked into a regular conversation. A code word can indicate to your parents that you would like them to pick you up but don't feel comfortable telling your peers that you want to leave. This is especially useful in risky situations.

- **Widen your social network:** It's a good idea to make friends with other teens from all aspects of your life. You could make friends at an extracurricular activity, during family activities, while taking part in volunteer work, at an afterschool job, etc. However, the people you spend time with should have similar morals and values to you. They should support you, speak up for you when you need support, and you should be able to do the same for them. Even having one person to stand with you against peer pressure can make it easier to resist.

- **Talk to a trusted family member or role model:** Never hesitate to ask for help from someone you trust, especially if the situation feels dangerous. Advice from a trusted adult, parent, caregiver, teacher, school counselor, or role model can help you feel better about your choices and help you prepare for peer pressure in future situations.

- **Listen to your gut:** If you feel uncomfortable, listen to your gut even if your friends seem okay with what's going on. When you physically feel like something is wrong, your brain is trying to tell you that the situation is potentially dangerous. Listen to this feeling! The more you listen to yourself and learn to trust what your mind and body are trying to tell you, the more self-reliant you become.

- **Plan for possible scenarios:** Sit down with your parents or caregivers to create a backup plan for possible situations you might encounter as you move through adolescence. This includes dangerous and safe situations like outings with friends, first dates, or even walking home by yourself. Planning ahead can help you prepare for possible dangers, so you always have a safe way out.

- **If you need a way out, use your parents:** If you don't want to do something, you don't have to do it. By this I mean your friends inviting you to a party where you know they will drink, use drugs, or make you feel uncomfortable. Decline the invitation by telling the other person you can't because your mom won't let you and you promised to help your dad with some chores. You could even say it's your aunt's birthday or you have to watch your younger sister.

Living a healthy lifestyle can be difficult when you are going through a period of drastic change, but it's not impossible. You have to be patient with yourself during this time too. Showing yourself forgiveness and compassion can take away some of the pressure that accompanies building healthy habits, but you also have to take responsibility because you are becoming more independent.

You are now at a stage in your life where you can start making your own decisions, so choose wisely and learn from your mistakes. However, your relationships are also a part of the many changes you experience as you enter puberty. Chapter 4 will help you better understand what these changes could look like and how you can cope with them.

NOTES TO SELF

Write your thoughts, feelings, comments and anything you need to get off your chest or just make notes. This is your book, your space, take control.

NOTES TO SELF

Write your thoughts, feelings, comments and anything you need to get off your chest or just make notes. This is your book, your space, take control.

Chapter 4:

Let's Talk About Your

Relationships

Some people come into our lives and quickly go. Some stay for a while, leave footprints on our hearts, and we are never, ever the same. –Flavia Weed

Adolescence is a time in your life when you begin figuring out who you are as you gain more independence. This change impacts your relationships, especially as your parents and friends are also experiencing their own changes as you get older. As scary as change can be, it allows you to become an independent young woman who can make her own decisions.

Before you reach this point, you are going to make mistakes, argue with the people you care about, have to solve problems, lose old friends, and make new ones. Having a better understanding of how adolescence can impact your relationships can prepare you for changes you might experience.

Relationships With Family Members

You physically and mentally change during adolescence. This triggers changes in your relationships with family members, no matter how close you are. Your family members, especially your parents and siblings, also experience their own changes. Your focus shifts and you begin to want more independence and privacy. Conflict and arguments may occur because your family believes if they can keep hold of their control, then your relationship with them doesn't have to change.

You are also figuring out that your parents or caregivers don't always know everything and can't solve every problem, so you begin to question them more too. You may rebel, fight back, or react instead of responding to problems. A lack of understanding by both parties, miscommunication, and difficulty accepting change can make adolescence a very difficult time for families, but it doesn't have to be that way.

If you and your parents or caregivers are willing to learn about the changes you could experience in your relationships, you can work together to overcome conflict in a way that strengthens your relationship.

Parents or Guardians

Throughout your life, your parents or caregivers act as your safe space. They provide you with support, safety, love, and acceptance—which is important during adolescence. They set rules, standards of behavior, and boundaries; however, you may have noticed that some of these rules and boundaries change as you get older. Parents or caregivers want you to stay safe and provide you with the best future they can. Unfortunately, it isn't always easy for you to see it this way, triggering arguments.

Remember that your parents are also experiencing change as you go from being their baby to a young woman. It can be hard for them to accept this change, especially in the beginning. They have to cope with their loss of control over you and your life because up until now, your parents were responsible for helping you choose your outfits, scheduling appointments and after-school activities, and general lifestyle choices. As you get older and gain more independence, you begin to take over these responsibilities. Many parents or caregivers find this hard to accept.

When you gain responsibility or get into arguments with your parents, you may also feel like you're not living up to their expectations. Some parents or caregivers may feel disappointed that you aren't following their plans for your future, but they need to accept that you are smart and capable, and want to follow your own plans for your future. These plans might change, but if your parents or caregivers can let go of their need to control every part of your life, they can go on this journey with you and provide you with the support and encouragement you need.

If they show interest in your plans, friends, or interests, reciprocate by opening up to them. Arguments and conflict occur for various reasons. Learning to solve problems together, compromising, and communicating will require hard work by you and your parents, but the effort is worth it. You can use the tips that follow to help you improve and maintain a healthy relationship with your parents:

- **Have one-on-one time:** Make an effort to spend time together so you can stay connected, have real conversations, share your problems and concerns, ask parents for advice, talk about your friends and share what's happening in your life, and just enjoy each other's company. Activities include going for a walk, working on a hobby or activity, watching a movie, listening to their stories, or baking together. You could also choose activities you both enjoy and switch between them.

- **Do family outings:** Each member of the family should be given the opportunity to choose an activity where you are all involved, like going to the zoo, the movie theater, grocery shopping, bowling, walks in the park, etc.

- **Agree to family rituals:** Cooking together, movie or game nights, baking together, and gardening are all potential daily or weekly activities you can do as a family to stay connected.

- **Abide by family rules:** If there are rules or consequences you feel are unfair, share your concerns with your parents or caregivers. In return for creating fair rules you all agree to, you have to make an effort to abide by them and accept the consequences should you break these rules. This includes owning up to bad behavior even when your parents or caregivers don't know about it. They will appreciate your honesty and it increases their trust in you. Having a safe space where you can negotiate rules so they are fair can not only reduce conflict in your household, but also increase your chances of remembering and adhering to these rules.

Siblings

If there is one person on this Earth that knows who you really are, it's your sibling. However, your relationship with them is also really complex and difficult for outsiders to understand. You might even have a relationship that constantly shifts between best friends and lifelong enemies. Of course, this relationship looks extremely different for all siblings. It's still important for you to remember that this relationship will change and that's okay.

Many times, siblings find that they become closer during adolescence because you can be yourself around them without having to pretend or feeling pressured to behave a specific way. You can share your worries and feelings with them without facing judgment, and they will give you advice too. Your sibling will always be your constant and give you the strength to live your own life. Unfortunately, you may still experience a few issues, including:

- **Sibling rivalry:** Siblings argue, but when you enter adolescence, these arguments may become more intense. Especially if you have different personalities and styles, and are different ages. Sometimes siblings don't get along. That's okay, but you should still be respectful and civil with each other because you are both people deserving of respect, regardless of your age or popularity status at school.

- **Envy:** If your sibling is older than you, you may be envious that they have more independence and privileges than you. Remind yourself that you will gain those privileges in a few years too.

Some siblings become jealous of the other because they are talented in a specific area—like art, music, or sport—and are constantly praised for it. This can impact your relationship and be hard to cope with. Remember that you are both unique individuals with your own set of talents and skills. You could ask your sibling to help you develop your skills or help you find your interest.

- **Bonding in crisis:** You will experience different crisis events throughout your life. You will see how your siblings overcome such events and learn that they are also great at providing you with the support you need.

- **Work on this friendship:** Every relationship in your life requires work, and while siblings are always there for each other, you have to work on this relationship. Communicate with each other, spend time together, solve problems, and work on your relationship.

- **Resolve fights:** While arguing with your sibling is normal, they are the one person who knows exactly what to say to hurt you deeply. You and your siblings have to actively work on solving problems together after taking time to calm down. Try to listen to each other's experiences and views, compromise, communicate honestly, and consider using problem-solving tools like writing your problems down.

- **Calm each other down:** You and your sibling can probably read each other's body language and facial expressions very clearly. Use this skill to help each other walk away from an argument or situation to calm down. Practice breathing together or talking out the problem before going back to the situation to solve it. Sometimes venting to your sibling—a person who won't judge you—can help you clear your mind and figure out how to resolve an argument.

Relationships With Friends

It's important to have friends throughout your life, but your friend group doesn't have to be big for your relationships to be meaningful or valuable. Friendship helps you build your social and emotional skills, while also teaching you how to be sensitive to other people's feelings, thoughts, and well-being. A good friend is one that supports you, shares your views and values, allows you to feel comfortable being yourself, gives you comfort and security, and is willing to experience new things with you without putting either of you in danger. They won't pressure or guilt you into doing anything you don't want to either. I have included a few tips for you to remember about friendship in the list that follows:

- **No friendship is perfect:** You will argue and get irritated with each other, and sometimes you won't agree, but that's normal. If your friendship is healthy, you will be able to share your thoughts and feelings with your friend in an honest way without worrying that your friendship will end. Being able to resolve conflicts together is also important and will strengthen your relationship. You should do this without trying to fix your friends; accept them for who they are.

- **Yo-yo friendships aren't healthy:** An unhealthy friendship occurs when your friend is really nice to you for a while before leaving you alone for no reason, and then shows up a few months later as if nothing happened. This is unfair to you and you should leave people who do this to you.

- **You won't always be included:** This happens for a number of reasons, like your friend making a mistake on their invites. If your friend is purposely excluding you, you don't need them. It's okay to cut out people who aren't putting in the same effort you are.

- **Not all friendships will last:** It's okay to be sad when your friendships end. Mourn your friendship, learn from it, and move on. You are resilient and you will make new friends.

- **There may be fights over boyfriends:** Don't allow boys to get in the way of your friendships because your friends will always be there to provide you with support, acceptance, strength, and love long after your relationship has ended.

- **Never compare friendships:** There is a big difference between fictional and real friendships. Remember that social media allows you to share only the exciting parts of your life that you want people to see, but that doesn't mean you or the other person are always happy and going out to socialize.

- **Some of your friends won't like each other:** Your friends won't always like each other and that's okay. Never try to force a friendship between your friends, but you should ensure they aren't being mean to each other either.

- **Some of your "friends" won't really be friends:** A friendship can be one-sided, and it can hurt. Allow yourself to move on to healthier relationships with people who put in as much effort as you do.

- **Don't allow friends to control you:** You are your own person, so stand up for yourself and be assertive. True friends won't try to control you or change who you are.

- **Friendships require work but are worth it:** You and your friends will have to resolve arguments, communicate honestly, and spend time together. You will both make mistakes and sometimes friends might accidentally hurt you, but working together to improve your friendship can help you enjoy each other's company and create a lasting friendship.

Your Relationship with Social Media

Social media is a big part of our lives and your real-life friendships may be replaced with online ones, especially after the COVID-19 pandemic. But you have to be careful. Social media exposes you to things that may cause you to hate how you look and act, pressure you to lose weight, or hurt your friendships.

As the presence of social media increases, mental health and satisfaction with life has decreased for many people, especially young girls (Perry, 2022: par. 3). Social media preys on young girls during a very vulnerable time of their life and can expose you to bullying and negativity. Even if this hasn't been your experience, you have to remain vigilant because it's easy to miss. According to Elsesser (2021: par. 6 to 15), social media puts you at an increased risk of:

- cyberbullying

- replacing your real-life friendships with online ones

- mental health issues like anxiety and depression

- developing an eating disorder or other body issues

- suicidal ideation

Fortunately, there are a number of ways you can build your own healthy social media habits, including:

- creating your own boundaries and respecting the boundaries of others in an online environment.

- talking to your parents or caregivers, siblings, or a counselor when you notice social media making you feel anxious or sad.

- becoming aware of the language you use when you are on social media, as well as how social media's language impacts your daily life.

- spending time away from social media.

Romantic Relationships

Entering adolescence and starting puberty means you may begin to become interested in romantic relationships. Some teenagers develop this interest earlier than other teens, while others only develop this interest later. However, some teens also aren't interested in having a romantic relationship. That's okay, but you should still understand how these relationships work and learn how to identify the signs of a toxic relationship because others may express romantic interest in you.

You may even develop an interest in other girls (known as "same-sex attraction") or an interest in both men and women (called "bisexuality"). These relationships work in a very similar way. Regardless of your interest, you should be clear about how you feel and who you are attracted to. Speak with an adult or mentor that you can trust, especially if you are confused.

It can be hard experiencing an attraction that doesn't match what you normally see in the media. Even if you are straight, it's normal to be curious, experiment, and explore. Accepting yourself for who you are is important, but you should also know the different stages of a typical teenage relationship.

Stages of Teenage Relationships

In general, there are six stages of dating for teenagers:

- **Crushing:** You start out admiring the person you are interested in, but neither of you knows the other is romantically interested.

- **Connecting:** You start interacting with the person you are interested in. This includes talking, flirting, and casual touches, like a hand on the arm. These interactions can occur in person, online, or at after school groups. It's normal to feel anxious or fear being rejected at this stage, especially if you aren't sure they share your interest.

- **Making the leap:** If they reciprocate your interest, your relationship will begin by letting the other person know you want to be in a romantic relationship. You will begin to date and spend more time together.

- **Settling into a relationship:** This is the longest stage of your relationship. You and your partner feel more comfortable with each other and continue spending time together. Your feelings may also become stronger, and you could decide to engage in and explore sexual activities.

- **Getting restless:** If you or your partner aren't ready to become serious, you may find yourself becoming irritated, attracted to other people, or feeling trapped. This is hard to accept, but teenagers are often at different stages of maturity which can affect their relationships.

- **Breaking up:** This is the hardest stage of your relationship, especially if it's your first relationship. A breakup can happen gradually or suddenly, in person or over text. You might withdraw so you can cry, get angry, and mourn your relationship. Allow yourself to feel your emotions, but know that your parents and friends are there to support you and provide you with unconditional love. If you are struggling with suicidal ideation or thoughts of self-harm, consider seeking professional help.

Developing an interest in dating can be something every parent dreads, but you may also feel anxious or awkward about your interest. Remember that it's normal to want to date and it can be good for you. Dating helps you develop your social skills and grow emotionally, but if you aren't interested in dating now, you can still develop these skills in your friendships. Take it slow. You don't need to rush into anything, especially if you aren't comfortable dating yet or becoming more serious about your partner. Communication and honesty will be very important here.

However, you also need to be aware of your expectations. Social media, tv series, and movies have an unrealistic representation of relationships, especially teen relationships. In reality, dating is awkward, and it might not meet your expectations. Although, social media and instant messaging do allow you to get to know your potential partner before you go on your first date. This can take away some of the awkwardness and anxiety, but you should also spend time in person.

When you do meet up, you should keep your family's safety rules in mind. Dating for girls, especially young girls, can be dangerous. You have to know how to stay safe while you are out in public and let your parents know where you are going and when you expect to be home. Your parents should also have your date and their parents' contact information.

You also have to know your boundaries (which I will discuss in more detail in Chapter 7) because some boys do try and push your boundaries and rush into things. That's not your fault. You are not responsible for a boy's actions. Understanding what you are comfortable with can help you speak up if they do try to push your boundaries. You should also have a trusted adult you can talk to. They can give you advice, help you understand your partner's words and behaviors, and you can confide in them if something does happen.

Signs of a Toxic or Unhealthy Relationship

A new relationship and the intense emotions that often accompany them can make it easy for you to miss the warning signs of a toxic partner. You may even dismiss these signs while your parents and friends express their concerns. You deserve better than being controlled, manipulated; or mentally, emotionally, or physically abused for the benefit of someone else. An unhealthy relationship can have a very big impact on your life and your future, especially future relationships.

If you are struggling to leave a relationship, don't feel safe, or feel uncomfortable, speak with someone you trust, like a parent, caregiver, counselor, psychologist, older sibling, or even a friend. Use the list of warning signs that follow to help you identify a toxic relationship. This list isn't comprehensive so I would suggest speaking with a counselor or doing your own research on toxic relationships:

- Changing your habits, behavior, likes, and dislikes for your boyfriend.

- Your boyfriend acts possessive, demands all your time, cuts you off from friends and family, is possessive, or is extremely jealous.

- A constant need to apologize.

- Difficulty explaining where you got injuries from.

- Your boyfriend doesn't allow you to pursue or work on your goals because he wants your focus to only be on him and his needs.

- You change your appearance for your boyfriend.

- He constantly has to know where you are, who you are with, and what you are doing.

- Your relationship becomes serious too quickly and you may feel uncomfortable or hesitant about it even though your boyfriend is happy.

- You don't want to spend time with your family anymore.

- Your personality changes.

- You constantly make excuses or apologize for your boyfriend's behavior.

A healthy relationship and a good partner bring out the best in you. Don't ever be afraid to break off a relationship with a toxic partner. Developing and changing relationships of all kinds are an important part of growing up. Real life is a lot more awkward and slow than it is in fiction. That's a good thing because it gives you and a potential partner time to build trust and communicate. So, what does a first date look like? Chapter 5 will help you understand the do's and don'ts of a first date.

NOTES TO SELF

Write your thoughts, feelings, comments and anything you need to get off your chest or just make notes. This is your book, your space, take control.

NOTES TO SELF

Write your thoughts, feelings, comments and anything you need to get off your chest or just make notes. This is your book, your space, take control.

Chapter 5:

Let's Talk About Your First

Date

I am a strong believer in kissing being very intimate, and the minute you kiss, the floodgates open for everything else. –Jennifer Lopez

You are probably excited about going on your first date, especially if you are interested in someone or your friends have had really good first dates already. However, your first date might be in a few months' time or even a few years. Some women start dating in their early teens, while others only begin dating in their 20s or 30s. That's nothing to be ashamed of or embarrassed about, but you should be prepared for the day you do decide to go on your first date.

Perhaps you've already been on your first date; the tips I've included in this chapter can be used for your first date with new potential partners. Remember that your first partner won't necessarily be your future spouse, and not every first date will lead to a second one. That's okay! Use each date you go on to grow, learn, and enjoy yourself. The tips in this chapter can help lessen some of the anxiety that accompanies a first date.

Before the Date

Checking in during your date, letting your parents know when you arrived or when you're on your way home, not being allowed to kiss on your first date, having a set curfew, or having one of your parents chaperone your date are some of the potential rules parents could set when their children begin dating. I know it feels unfair or like your parents are being overdramatic, but they have put these rules in place to keep you safe. Respect these rules and adhere to them. There will be time to hold hands, kiss, and spend time alone with your partner later. If your partner truly cares about and respects you, they will also adhere to these rules.

The modern dating world is just as terrifying for parents as it is for young girls because your gender and age can, unfortunately, put you in danger (I'll talk about this more in later chapters). If you and your partner adhere to these rules, your parents or caregivers can learn to trust you both. They may even relax their rules to give you some freedom, but you shouldn't take advantage of this. You will probably be nervous or anxious before your first date. But your date probably feels the same way! So how can you prepare for your date in a way that lessens some of your anxiety?

- Know or have a plan. Preparing for your date is key. Even if your date is planning what you will do, ask them where you will be going, what activities you'll do, if you're going to grab something to eat, do you need to bring anything specific, will they drop you off, and what time your date will end. This allows your parents, caregivers, or siblings to know where you are, what you're doing, who will be there, and what time they can expect you home before they should begin to worry.

- Have an escape plan. Don't ever ignore your gut! If you feel uncomfortable, if your date creeps you out, if you don't feel safe, or if something feels off, have a safe word that you can text to your parents, sibling, friend, or caregiver so they can come and fetch you. For example, you could excuse yourself to the bathroom and give them a call or send a text message with the safe word so they can call you with a fake emergency that means they need to pick you up. This plan will look different for everyone.

- Plan your outfit. The clothes you wear should suit the activity. For example, heels aren't appropriate if you go paintballing or bowling.

While you should definitely dress nicer than you would at school, you should wear comfortable clothing that makes you feel happy and confident in yourself. This means you can walk, talk, eat, and breathe in your clothes. Knowing the plan for your date can also help you figure out what kind of clothes you should wear.

- What are the possibilities? This includes where you're going to eat and the activities you'll do. After all, letting your date know *after* sitting down at the restaurant that you're allergic to or don't like their food can make it awkward. If you have physical limitations, like asthma, that make things like physical activities a bit riskier, your date should also be informed. You should also prepare for possibilities like wanting to go home early because the date isn't going well, or you don't feel comfortable.

- Don't plan on romance. There will be plenty of time for romance in the future, but first dates can be really awkward when you're both really nervous about it going well. Go slow, focus on enjoying yourself, and be yourself.

- Create a positive mindset. The anxiety that accompanies a first date is not enjoyable. Put on your favorite music while you get ready, meditate for a few minutes, or ask your friend or sibling to help you get ready so they can encourage you and help you feel more comfortable.

- What physical contact are you comfortable with? It's okay if you don't kiss, hold hands, or even hug on the first date. These can be really intimate acts, especially if you've never dated before. You also don't know what kind of physical affection your partner is comfortable with. Many teens avoid these big moves until their third date at least so they can get to know their partner and what they are comfortable with first. Don't do anything you aren't ready for. A good partner will respect this.

During the Date

Now that you have a plan of action, it's time to go on your date. The list that follows includes a few tips to help you feel more confident and comfortable on your date.

- When your date picks you up or you meet at the agreed spot, give them a brief, but warm, "Hello." You could smile or give them a brief hug, but this will depend on how well you already know each other and whether you've met in person before or not. Don't overthink it, your date is probably just as nervous as you are.

- First dates are awkward! They are about getting to know each other while avoiding sensitive or invasive topics like politics, religion, or any other sensitive subjects. Keep the conversation light by asking your date questions that help the conversation flow. Allow your date to do the same, especially if you have a shared interest that you can bond over.

- Offer to split the check. Even if your date insists on paying, it's a good idea to offer to share the costs or even cover the tip. You could also offer to pay for dessert later. When choosing something to eat, don't pick the most expensive meal. Choose something in the same price range as what your date orders.

- If you feel a need for physical contact on your date, remember the rules you set about this contact before your date and stick to them.

- Always remember your escape plan. Don't feel guilty or stay out of obligation because your date is paying or bought you a gift. They lose any date or friend privileges the moment they disrespect your boundaries, make you feel unsafe, or expect something from you that you don't feel comfortable being part of, like kissing, breaking any rules or laws, or having sex on the first date.

After the Date

You and your date are probably a bit more comfortable with each other now. The tips that follow can help you act casual, while also letting your date know you had fun.

- After your date drops you off at home or your parents pick you up, you could send them a quick and simple thank you for the date text. If you had fun, you could also tell them you enjoyed yourself and would like to do it again soon. If you didn't have fun but continued with the date, you could simply thank them. If they ask if you want to go on another date but you didn't enjoy yourself, politely decline. Always be honest, but don't send your date a long message either.

- Don't stalk your date. It might feel tempting to find them on social media and obsess over their pictures after your date, but you need to ignore this feeling. Stick to a simple and brief, "Thank you," text.

- Be careful about your expectations. Even if you enjoyed yourself and the other person had fun, they may have decided you're both better off as friends than romantic partners. Respect each other's boundaries and feelings. It might not feel like it now, but you will find yourself going on another date with a person you can be yourself around without feeling judged in the future.

Rejection, awkwardness, and anxiety are just some of the uncomfortable feelings you will experience while dating. Not every first date will lead to a second one either. Sometimes, people work better as friends than they do as romantic partners. This can hurt when you really care about the other person, but trying to fake something (especially feelings) that doesn't exist will only hurt you both in the long run.

Use your first date to help you get to know the other person, grow your own communication and people skills, and enjoy yourself. It's always great when a date works out, but there are new pressures and expectations that accompany dating someone for a long period of time. Chapter 6 will talk about the pressure that you as a young girl will face in regard to sex, what sex is, and what you can expect if you do decide to engage in this activity.

NOTES TO SELF

Write your thoughts, feelings, comments and anything you need to get off your chest or just make notes. This is your book, your space, take control.

NOTES TO SELF

Write your thoughts, feelings, comments and anything you need to get off your chest or just make notes. This is your book, your space, take control.

Chapter 6:

Let's Talk About Sex

Expired condoms are like nuclear waste: There's nothing sensible you can do with it. –Andrew Smith

Sexual intercourse, or "sex" as you probably know it, can be for pleasure and reproduction. You might be curious about what sex is and how it feels, but this activity can be intense because you and your partner connect on a physical and emotional level in a way that's difficult to prepare for. Sex also comes with risks such as pregnancy, sexually transmitted diseases (STDs), HIV, etc.

You and your partner need to prepare properly before having sex, including using protection and birth control, as well as being respectful of each other's sexual boundaries. You have the right to change your mind at any moment. A respectful partner will be willing to wait and will respect your boundaries, listen to you when you say "no," and won't try to pressure you into having sex. As important as it is to understand what sex is and how to keep yourself safe, you first need to understand your anatomy better as the female and male reproductive organs are quite different.

Understanding Anatomy

Learning about sex and the reproductive system might make you feel awkward, especially if you haven't learned about it in school yet, but you don't have to feel embarrassed or ashamed. Your body has the ability to create life and, while this isn't easy and can be dangerous to your health, your body still deserves to be taken care of and respected. You can only do that, however, if you have a better understanding of your anatomy.

Female Anatomy

Breasts are often considered sexual organs, mainly by men, but they are actually secondary sex characteristics. The female reproductive system is mainly found within your body. The external part of this system is located between your legs, starting with the "vulva" (meaning "covering") which covers the opening to your vagina and internal reproductive organs. The mons pubis is the fleshy area located just above your vaginal opening and is surrounded by two skin flaps, called the "labia."

A small sensory organ is found where these two folds join and is known as the "clitoris." Located between your labia are the openings to your urethra (the channel that transports urine outside your body) and your vagina. The outer layer of your labia and mons pubis will be covered by pubic hair as your body sexually matures (*Female reproductive system*, 2019: par. 7-8).

The hymen is very thin and is made up of a skin-like tissue that partly covers the opening to your vagina, but the hymen forms differently in every female. It can stretch or tear during your first-time having sex or even during a physical activity like horse riding or bike riding.

Your vagina (a muscular, hollow tube extending from your vaginal opening to your uterus) is part of your internal reproductive system. It's also the channel through which menstrual blood leaves your body, where a man's penis is inserted during sexual intercourse, where a tampon is inserted, and the channel where a baby would leave your uterus (also called the "womb") through childbirth (*Female reproductive system*, 2019: par. 8-16).

The cervix is the point where your vagina connects to your uterus. While it's a very small opening, it has thick, strong walls to accommodate a baby passing through. At the upper corners of your uterus are two tubes, called the "fallopian tubes," that connect the uterus to your ovaries. Ovaries produce, store, and release your eggs and also produce the female sex hormones estrogen and progesterone (*Female reproductive system*, 2019: par. 17-21).

Male Anatomy

The reproductive organs of boys can be found both inside and outside of their pelvis. This system is made up of their penis, testicles, and duct system (consisting of the epididymis and vas deferens), and accessory glands (made up of the seminal vesicles and prostate gland). The testicles are responsible for making the male hormones, specifically testosterone. Sperm are also produced in the testicles and are transported via the epididymis and vas deferens. The epididymis and testicles are contained in a pouch-like structure, called the "scrotum," found hanging outside the pelvis to regulate its temperature.

The channel that carries the sperm, found in a fluid called "semen," is known as the urethra and is the same channel through which urine leaves the body through the penis. Made up of the shaft and glans, also called the "head," the glans have a small opening through which semen and urine exit the body. All boys are also born with a fold of skin that covers the end of their penis, called the "foreskin," but it's sometimes removed at birth for religious purposes even though this procedure is not medically necessary (*Male reproductive system*, 2019: par. 7-16).

It's Not Always Straightforward

You have probably already realized that gender and sexual identity aren't as simple as male and female, straight or gay. Many people have different gender identities and sexual orientations that often fall under the LGBTQIA+ community. For example, a person who identifies as nonbinary doesn't relate to she/her or he/him pronouns and gender expectations because they might not feel comfortable trying to conform to the gender binary.

Instead, they use they/them pronouns and wear clothing they feel comfortable in and like to wear, regardless of gender. You or your partner may even fall into this category.

Your relationship may also look slightly different as you and your partner settle into a companionship that respects both your identities and needs without pressuring either of you or making you uncomfortable.

Gender and sexual identity are very diverse topics that you should do your own research on, especially if your partner isn't a straight boy, or you get butterflies when spending time with the pretty girl in your art class but not when the hot boy all the girls fawn over asks you out.

Resisting Pressure to Have Sex

As soon as you enter adolescence and begin puberty, you may start to notice an increase in pressure to have sex and engage in sexual activities. Girls especially feel this pressure, but you should never feel or be forced to have sex. It can be hard when your partner or friends pressure you to engage in this intimate act, but you can resist them by discussing the pressures you might face, talking about your concerns about having sex, identifying your internal pressures to keep up with friends, and working with a trusted adult to talk about and practice what to do if someone does try to force you to have sex.

Resisting this pressure is hard when you want to fit in, but you shouldn't do it just to keep up with the crowd. Avoiding drugs and alcohol (notorious for lowering a person's inhibitions), surrounding yourself with friends who don't take sex lightly and encourage you to focus on your schoolwork, and having a number of planned responses to such pressure can help you resist. However, if you are ever forced to have sex, please remember that you are not to blame and you should not blame yourself for the actions of others.

Talk to a trusted adult who can help you move forward. The table that follows includes a list of possible phrases someone might use to convince you to have sex. I have included potential responses, but you can work with a trusted adult to create your own list of responses and practice them (*Helping teens resist sexual pressure*, 2009: par.20-28).

Manipulative Phrase	Potential Response
"Let's have sex, I know you want to!"	"No, no I don't! What part of 'no' don't you understand?"
"I don't understand why you won't have sex with me?"	"I don't want to." You don't have to provide them with any further explanation. "No" is always enough.
"Let's go back to your house since your parents are out all night."	Blame your parents! "We can't go back to my house. My parents refuse to let me have boys over, especially if they're not home." You could also lie and say that an aunt who would enforce this rule is waiting for you.
"Why are you saying "no" when we've had sex before?"	"I am allowed to change my mind at any stage. It's my body, my life, and my

	choice." You could also add that you'd prefer to wait until you're older before having sex again.
"I'll break up with you if you don't have sex with me."	"I don't want to date you if I have to sleep with you even after telling you 'no.' I guess this is goodbye then."
"Aw, but everybody does it!"	"I'm not everybody. Anyway, half the kids who say they have sex haven't even done it before."
"If you loved me, you would have sex with me."	"If you loved me, you wouldn't pressure me into doing something I'm not ready to do and have clearly said 'no' to."

Remember to be assertive, firm, and confident when saying "no" and turning the other person down. If you are scared, they will leave you, remember that you don't need anyone in your life who tries to manipulate you into doing something you don't want to because people like that don't really care about or respect you.

How Do You Know When You're Ready?

Sex not only involves your body, but also includes connecting to your partner on a more emotional level. Your first time, and every time after that, can have an impact on you that affects how you feel about and see yourself, as well as your life. There are a number of things to consider when thinking about having sex for the first time. When you do reach the point in your relationship where you feel ready to have sex, talk not only with your partner, but also with a trusted adult or parent, and your healthcare provider. Protecting against sexually transmitted illnesses (STIs) (discussed in Chapter 8) and preventing pregnancy is important for having safe sex. Your healthcare provider can help you figure out how to do this in a way that suits your needs and lifestyle.

When deciding you are ready to have sex, ensure you're making an informed decision. The teenage years can be a confusing time when your hormones are clashing with your feelings for someone. The right time to have sex is different for everyone too, and you might only want to have sex once you are engaged or after marriage when you're older. Having sex is a personal choice and **no one** can make that choice for you.

Once you have discussed your decision with a trusted adult and healthcare provider, you should also speak with your partner. They might not be ready for sex yet.

If they are, you should both discuss whether it's the right decision, what your and your partner's sexual history looks like (even if neither of you has had sex before) and if they do have a sexual history, you should both undergo a sexual health screening for STIs, HIV, etc. This helps decrease the risk of either partner accidentally transmitting a virus or disease that could have long-term health effects. This should also lead to a conversation about the contraceptives you will both use. However, you and your partner should also consider whether:

- you both feel comfortable and safe around each other.

- you both feel confident and comfortable being yourselves when you are together.

- there is a bond of mutual respect and trust.

- you can openly and confidently discuss your fears and dreams with each other.

- your partner dismisses you and your feelings or makes you feel uncomfortable at any point in your relationship.

If you hesitated or said "no" to any of the above points, then you aren't ready to have sex. Having sex at a young age involves a number of risks and you shouldn't rush or put yourself in a situation you don't want to be in just to keep up with your friends or make your partner happy.

What Does "Virginity" Mean?

Virginity has many definitions that often depend on your beliefs, religion, values, and culture. In general, "virginity" is described as your hymen remaining intact, but the hymen develops differently in different women. Some women aren't born with a hymen, while activities like horse riding, riding a bike, and gymnastics could break the hymen of a woman who has never been sexually active. As such, a virgin could also be defined as a woman who has never been sexually penetrated. With so many different definitions available, reflect on your own beliefs and decide for yourself how you want to define your virginity.

If your hymen remains intact and is only broken after you have sex for the first time, you may experience a bit of pain and there might be blood. Don't panic, it's normal. Not all women bleed when their hymen is broken, but some women do bleed when they have sex for the first time due to minor tearing caused by your partner's penis when they enter you for the first time.

This is also normal as you've never had anything inserted there before—except maybe a tampon or your fingers during masturbation. Place a towel underneath you if you're worried about blood. You could also use a water-based lubricated condom to make the entry and exit of your partner's penis smoother.

Having Sex for the First Time

Having sex, especially for the first time, will be awkward. It's nothing like the movies or books. You and your partner are exploring a completely new aspect of your relationship that includes getting to know each other's bodies more intimately. You are literally getting up close and personal with your partner so awkward moments like sneezing, coughing, or even farting might occur. Don't rush either. Take your time to learn what you both like.

When you decide you are ready to have sex for the first time, it should be with someone you really love and care about. You and your partner need to be there for each other before and after sex too. This means being comfortable with each other and being able to clearly and honestly communicate without fearing judgment or criticism. You should also avoid porn as your teacher. Porn isn't real life; it's violent, aggressive, direct, and could cause you pain.

As such, communication will be very important for you and your partner. If you're ready to have sex, tell your partner. If they're also ready, you can start planning your first time together. Don't let it stress you out either. This can make it harder for you both to enjoy yourselves and reach orgasm; as such, foreplay will play an important role. Start by setting the mood. This prepares you both for sex by building anticipation. This can lead on to foreplay, which is important because women can struggle to reach orgasm, especially when they are stressed out or anxious.

Ensuring you are both alone and won't be disturbed can help with this anxiety too, allowing you both to enjoy being with each other. When you reach orgasm during sexual intercourse, you will experience a release of tension accompanied by intense pleasure. So don't fake it. You might not have an orgasm during your first time, but that doesn't mean you can't enjoy being with each other. Although, communicating to your partner what you enjoy can guide them in figuring out how to help you reach orgasm. Open and honest communication is critical for both partners to enjoy themselves, but you also have to consider what type of contraceptives you will both use.

Types of Contraceptives

As a girl, you have a wide variety of birth control options available. While some methods are more effective or useful than others at protecting against unwanted pregnancy and STIs, the method you choose to use will be personal. I recommend speaking with your gynecologist or healthcare provider as soon as you feel ready and comfortable having sex but before your first time. A qualified healthcare provider can tell you what contraceptives are available to you; which one will be best for you and your current health status, age, and lifestyle choices, as well as any possible side effects. Although, you have to remember that the type of contraceptive you use may change over the years to better suit your and your partner's needs.

While the list of contraceptives discussed in this section is not exhaustive, I have provided you with the basic information you need to help you make the right decision about birth control for you.

For Boys: Condoms

You've probably heard about condoms already. They are male contraceptives that can be used to reduce your risk of pregnancy and the transmission of STDs, STIs, and HIV. However, condoms are only 98% effective and can break or be corroded depending on how they are stored and unwrapped, and the types of lube used (Benveniste, 2022: par.23).

While you do get female condoms, they are rare and should never be used at the same time as male condoms as they could tear, rendering them useless. Latex condoms that have been designed for men should be stored in a cool, dry place, out of direct sunlight. Water-based lube is safe to use with these types of condoms and you should never use a condom that has passed its expiry date.

You should also use a new condom every time you have sex. If you or your partner think the condom broke, your partner should withdraw immediately so they can replace their condom with a new one. Using a condom may seem intimidating, but there are instructions on its packaging, and you could practice using one by placing it on a banana.

For Girls: Birth Control

Various types of birth control medications, devices, and methods exist, but the one you use will depend on a number of factors. Due to the wide variety of birth control strategies available, I recommend speaking with your healthcare provider or making use of the services of an organization like Planned Parenthood. There is no single "best method" of birth control because every woman is so different. As such, you should consider a few factors when talking about your options with your healthcare provider:

- Are you considering having children now or in the future (certain birth control methods can last between a few months to a year or more)?

- What type of birth control is best for preventing pregnancy?

- Which birth control method can prevent the transmission of STDs, STIs, and HIV?

- Due to current or past health issues—or underlying medical conditions—which birth control strategy does your healthcare provider recommend?

- What are the possible side effects of these options?

- What are the possible benefits in addition to preventing pregnancy or STDs, like managing acne or heavy periods?

- Do you need a prescription to use this type of birth control?

While these are only some of the factors you should consider, you have to remember that even the most effective method of birth control can fail. The list that follows provides you with a brief overview of some of the types of birth control you could consider (*Birth control methods*, 2022: par. 16-20).

- **Barrier methods:** A type of birth control that has to be replaced and used every time you have sex. These methods include cervical caps, condoms, sponges, and diaphragms.

- **Long-acting reversible contraceptives (LARC methods):** Your healthcare provider will insert this type of birth control into your body, so you don't have to remember to take a pill or shot. Intrauterine devices and hormonal implants are examples of LARC methods and could last between 3 to 10 years, but should be regularly checked to ensure they are still working.

- **Natural rhythm methods:** When you don't regularly use a birth control device or medication. Instead, you avoid sex or only use your birth control medication or device during your fertile window (the time of the month you are most likely to get pregnant and occurs during your ovulation period). This window is unique to all women.

- **Short-acting hormonal methods:** Prescribed by your healthcare provider, this type of birth control has to be taken either every day or every month. This method includes a patch, vaginal ring, pill, shot, or mini pills.

Types of Sex

There are many different types of sex; however, sex has a different meaning for everyone. This definition can depend on your religion, beliefs, morals, and what you have already been taught or learned about sex. While the list that follows explains some of the common forms this activity takes, you should always remember that sex should feel good and be comfortable for both you and your partner. If you experience pain at any stage, listen to your body and stop immediately.

- **Foreplay:** Activities that act as a type of preparation and usually occur before sex, even if you and your partner don't have sex. This can include cuddling, kissing, touching each other, or talking.

- **Masturbation:** Using your fingers or sex toys to stimulate your genitals in a way that will produce an orgasm and bring you pleasure.

- **Dry humping or genital rubbing:** When you and your partner rub your genitals against each other, or you rub your genitals against their leg or hand while wearing clothes to produce pleasure and stimulate an orgasm.

- **Oral sex:** Also known as "eating out" and "going down" when performed on a woman or a "blow job" when experienced by a man, this is when a person uses their mouth to stimulate their partner's genitals.

- **Vaginal sex:** When a penis enters a vagina. You can get pregnant or an STD if you don't use appropriate protection, like a condom.

- **Anal sex:** When a penis enters an anus. Not everyone enjoys this type of sex and if you are uncomfortable, you don't have to try it. Don't allow your partner to pressure or bully you into doing it.

While not all adults may feel comfortable discussing sex or answering questions about it, you should continue doing your own research on the topic (using reliable sources, not porn) so that you can prepare yourself for when you do decide to have sex. If something were to happen and your partner or another person forces themself on you sexually, you have to remember that you are not to blame. This leads us to the topic of "consent." Chapter 7 will help you better understand what sexual consent is, why it's so important, and how you can set your sexual boundaries.

NOTES TO SELF

Write your thoughts, feelings, comments and anything you need to get off your chest or just make notes. This is your book, your space, take control.

NOTES TO SELF

Write your thoughts, feelings, comments and anything you need to get off your chest or just make notes. This is your book, your space, take control.

Chapter 7:

Let's Talk About Consent

Consent is very sexy. There is nothing hotter than being asked, "Can I touch you here?" or "Do you want me inside you?" –
Glenda Love

You may have already heard of the term "consent," but not many people know what it is. Consent is when you explicitly and verbally express your enthusiastic permission for someone to touch you or engage in an activity, like sex, with you. You might be thinking, *it's not very sexy if your partner has to ask consent for every activity you engage in.* In reality, asking for your partner's consent—especially in a sexual situation—is not only vital, but also enjoyable.

Some partners even use consent for three things: Ensuring their partner is still comfortable with the activity they are engaging in, gaining permission to continue the activity (especially if it takes a new direction), and as a form of foreplay. As such, before engaging in any activity with your partner, they should ask for your consent just as you should ask for theirs. Consent is always reciprocal.

What Is Consent?

Consent gives you the right to feel safe while being pleasured by someone and awarding your partner with the same opportunity and respect. But it's not always as simple as saying "yes" or "no" to an activity. While verbal consent is the most common form of consent, the person who is conducting the pleasurable activity (like taking off clothes, touching your body, or even kissing you) should also be aware of their partner's body language. Non-verbal cues that indicate a partner isn't comfortable to include them trying to avoid the touch, leaning away, or tensing up, to name a few. True consent includes a confident and enthusiastic "yes," comfortable and relaxed body language, and positive responses to questions like

- Is it okay if I touch you here?

- Are we moving too fast?

- Are you enjoying yourself?

- Are you sure you're still okay with [activity you are currently engaging in]?

If you are the one pleasuring your partner, you should also check in with yourself using the same strategies and questions. Maybe your partner is ready to move things forward, but you aren't comfortable with it yet. That's okay! You have the right to change your mind at any stage of sex, without feeling guilty about it, because you are allowed to feel safe, pleasured, and comfortable at the same time. You might feel uncertain and nervous when engaging in sexual activities; tell your partner! Open and honest communication is important! A "yes" to one activity is not a "yes" to another one. Embracing and practicing consent in your relationship is essential for respectful, healthy, and safe sexual experiences.

What Isn't Consent?

You also have to remember that you **cannot** give consent if someone pressures you through verbal or physical threats and force, if you are under the legal age of sexual consent, you have ingested any type of alcohol or drugs, you don't completely understand the sexual activity they want you to take part in or its consequences, or you are asleep, semiconscious, unconscious, or irrational. You also have to remember that even if a person is flirting or wearing revealing or sexy clothing, they still haven't consented to an activity.

Setting and Enforcing Sexual Boundaries

To fully enjoy yourself, especially in a situation where you are being pleasured, you shouldn't have to worry about the other person violating or crossing your sexual boundaries. Boundaries are invisible lines that separate what you are and aren't comfortable with. This includes what you do and don't like in *any* situation in your life.

Everyone has different personal and sexual boundaries. For example, some people are huggers, while others don't like being hugged by just anyone. This is known as a "personal boundary." Boundaries deserve to be respected no matter what. But your partner won't know what your boundaries are unless you tell them. This is why I keep placing an emphasis on *open* and *honest* communication. It's the only way for partners to know what the other needs and dislikes.

Neither of you are mind readers. If you aren't comfortable with your partner doing something—even if you weren't originally aware this would cross one of your boundaries—tell them! Even if the activity you are currently engaging in has to stop. Instead, you can take part in an activity you are both comfortable with. Sexual boundaries include:

- **How others can see you:** Are you comfortable with your partner seeing you naked or only in your underwear? Maybe you don't want your partner to take their pants off but you're comfortable if they remove their shirt.

- **How you should be treated sexually:** This includes how you prefer to be touched. Some people are okay with being touched over their clothes, but not underneath (skin-to-skin contact). Maybe your partner isn't comfortable being touched on a specific area of their body.

- **What you're comfortable doing with others:** You've probably unconsciously noticed that you're okay with your best friend hugging you, but your acquaintance from class isn't allowed to hug you because it makes you uncomfortable. This is one type of activity boundary. In terms of sex, you might be comfortable receiving oral sex from your partner, but you don't feel comfortable giving it.

These are just some basic examples of possible boundaries you may have, especially when it comes to sexual activities. As awkward as you might feel setting your boundaries at first, you have to set them with your partner as soon as possible. It's easy to get lost in a haze of hormones, but that also means it's easy to do something you'll regret or that could hurt you.

How to Set Boundaries

Communication, trust, and respect are vital for setting and reinforcing sexual boundaries with your partner. Start by having an open and honest conversation with your partner **before** you engage in any physical activities, including holding hands, hugging, or kissing. You should also notice whether your partner is trying to push your boundaries or doesn't respect them. Reinforce your boundaries by explicitly and firmly stating that you aren't comfortable with what they are doing, and you want them to stop it right now.

Sexual relationships are dynamic, and miscommunications do happen. That's why you could restate and reinforce your boundary if a miscommunication does happen. If they continue crossing your boundaries, remove yourself from the situation in a way that is safe. For example, you could excuse yourself to the bathroom, but call a trusted adult to pick you up instead; flag down a friend using your agreed upon emergency signal or word if you are at a party; or you could immediately leave if you feel comfortable and safe enough to do so.

In situations where a partner refuses to respect your boundaries, even after you have reinforced them, and regardless of how small your boundary may be, you should think about breaking up with them. A relationship with someone who can't respect something as simple as a boundary does not and will not respect you. That's not a healthy, safe, or consensual relationship and you deserve better.

You don't have the sexual experience needed to go, "I like this exact activity, but not this one." That's nothing to be ashamed of. You can set a new boundary at any moment and if your partner respects and trusts you, they will respect your new boundary no matter how sudden it may seem. That's why it's also important to continuously ask for consent. You get to decide what happens to, and what you do with, your body.

It's your choice and your right because you are not an inanimate object that others can use and abuse for their own pleasure or needs. But sex also comes with additional risks such as pregnancy and STDs. Chapter 8 will discuss these topics in more detail so you can learn how to lower your risk.

NOTES TO SELF

Write your thoughts, feelings, comments and anything you need to get off your chest or just make notes. This is your book, your space, take control.

NOTES TO SELF

Write your thoughts, feelings, comments and anything you need to get off your chest or just make notes. This is your book, your space, take control.

Chapter 8:

Let's Talk About Pregnancy and STIs

I get tested for HIV twice a year... One has to be socially aware. It's part of being a decent human to be tested for STDs. It's just disgusting behavior when people don't. It's so irresponsible. —
Scarlett Johansson

It's easy for the adults in your life to tell you not to have sex until you're an adult or married, but in the end, the decision is yours. That's why I want you to understand what a healthy relationship looks like, how you can protect yourself mentally and physically, and the possible risks involved. Many teenagers don't have sex until later in their lives, but regardless of your age, you should be able to make informed decisions.

You don't need to have sex to successfully connect with and be intimate with your partner, but many teens want to experience this activity to understand why adults, the media, and society make such a big fuss over it. Sex comes with many risks, especially for women:

Pregnancy and sexually transmitted diseases (STDs) are the two main risks that can change your entire life.

Unplanned Teenage Pregnancy

Unplanned pregnancy occurs when you and your partner have unprotected sex, meaning you had sex without using a contraceptive, resulting in the fertilization of a female egg by a male sperm cell. The best way to avoid potential pregnancy is to avoid having sex, but contraceptives can help you lower your risk of getting pregnant. However, the incorrect use of any type of contraceptive, faulty contraceptive devices or implants, rape, or a ripped condom are all possible ways you could accidentally become pregnant no matter how careful you are.

It only takes one time. In such cases, an emergency contraceptive—which can be bought over the counter, without a prescription—could be used. This form of contraception can be taken up to five days after having unprotected sex. As your period can be unpredictable in the first few years of adolescence, you may also find it difficult to tell if you are pregnant (should this happen to you).

While a potential pregnancy is commonly associated with a missed period, possible accompanying symptoms include nausea or vomiting, sore nipples and/or breasts, frequent urination, unexplained mood swings, an intense aversion to certain foods, unexplained weight gain, fatigue, lightheadedness, and a swelling belly. If you suspect you are pregnant, I would recommend speaking with a trusted adult, counselor, school nurse, or healthcare provider so they can help you figure out if you are pregnant or not.

An at-home pregnancy test, bought from your local pharmacy or grocery store, can help you determine if you're pregnant or not too. While these tests have become more accurate and trustworthy over the years, a blood test would be more accurate and could help you detect a possible pregnancy up to a week earlier than an at-home test.

Increased Risk of Complications in Teenage Pregnancies

If you do accidentally become pregnant, you should be aware of the potential risks you face as a pregnant teen before making a decision about what to do about your pregnancy. Even though modern medicine has made great strides over the years, pregnancy is still an incredibly risky time for women and teen mothers face a number of unique risks.

Lack of Prenatal Care

Pregnant women require special care for themselves and their unborn babies. This includes specific vitamins that are essential for decreasing the risk of birth defects in your baby. Prenatal care aims to detect potential medical problems in you and your baby, deal with these complications as they arise, and monitor your baby's growth.

Feeling Isolated and Alone

If you feel like you can't tell your parents that you're pregnant, you're scared to tell them, or they react negatively, you may feel isolated, scared, and alone. You need support from the people you care about to get through pregnancy. Being pregnant isn't easy and while it's possible to have a healthy, full-term pregnancy and go on to raise a happy family, it can be harder to do it when you feel like you're alone.

Premature Birth

A woman is normally pregnant for 40 weeks, called a "full-term pregnancy." If your baby is born before 37 weeks, they are considered premature and are at a higher risk of cognitive, respiratory, and other problems. Premature labor also poses a threat to your health.

Low Birth Weight

When a baby weighs less than they should, they don't have enough time to grow properly in your womb. These babies often need to be placed on a ventilator to help with their breathing—one possible complication of low birth weight.

High Blood Pressure

There is a higher risk of high blood pressure in pregnant teens. High blood pressure puts you at risk of premature labor and developing conditions like "preeclampsia," a dangerous medical condition where your high blood pressure, increased protein in your urine, and swelling of your hands and face puts you at risk of complications such as potential organ damage. This condition can also impact your baby's growth.

Sexually Transmitted Diseases

When you have sex while you are pregnant, STDs become a big concern because they can also affect your baby and cause unnecessary complications to arise. Using a latex condom can decrease this risk.

Postpartum Depression

All women who have just given birth are at risk of postpartum depression, but as a teen, you are at a higher risk. Postpartum depression is depression that begins after you've given birth and can become quite severe, posing a danger to you and your baby if you don't get help. You need to speak with your healthcare provider, counselor, or someone else you trust if you begin to feel down and sad.

What Are Your Options?

If you accidentally become pregnant, you could decide to keep your baby and raise them, give them up for adoption, or get an abortion. You should tell your baby's father that you're pregnant and keep them updated on the decision you make. Pregnancy is a terrifying time for both partners.

As teens, hearing your partner is pregnant might cause them to run because they don't know how to handle this sudden responsibility, but they could also surprise you and decide to stay and support you. Either way, the final decision is up to you because it's **your** body that has to go through with the risk of pregnancy and your life will change the most after the birth.

Do your research and find all the facts so you can make an informed decision that is best for you and your future. Remember that children are a lifelong commitment. You can't wake up one day and decide you don't want to do it anymore. This is a big decision so counseling could help you better understand what your options are, how they could impact you, and help you figure out what the best option is.

Keeping the Baby

The movies and social media make raising a baby look easy and fun, but in reality, there is a LOT of hard work, sleepless nights, and little to no breaks if you don't have a support system. You also need to account for your current responsibilities like school, work, and extracurricular activities.

Raising a baby requires a support network, preparation, and money, and it's a lifelong commitment. You have to decide how you're going to support yourself and your baby, whether you can provide for their basic and medical needs, how will you feed and clothe them, whether you will carry on with school, is your partner going to be involved and contribute, what will your family do, and are you prepared for the stress and time commitment parenting requires?

These are just some of the questions you need to answer before making your final decision about keeping your baby.

Adoption

Adoption is a great option if you can't raise your baby yourself but don't want to get an abortion. An open adoption allows you to remain involved in your child's life—to a certain degree—but it still isn't easy. While many women don't regret giving their babies up for adoption, they still experienced a sense of grief and loss.

You have to research the possible adoption agencies available in your state and what services they offer. Remember that speaking with them to find out more about the adoption process, your rights, and how the process works don't mean you have decided to give your baby up for adoption. You still have time to think through your decision.

Abortion

Deciding to get an abortion is not a decision that is made lightly, but sometimes it's the best option. It's easy to judge a person until you are in their shoes. Pregnant people all have vastly different reasons for getting an abortion. Some aren't ready to have a baby for physical, mental, and medical reasons.

Other individuals become pregnant through violent situations like rape, and some women are experiencing medical issues that put their own health and life in danger if they were to go through with the pregnancy. More than 95% of the women who have chosen to get an abortion don't regret it (*What to do if you're a teenager and pregnant: Your 3 options*, 2017: par. 42).

However, abortion can have a major impact on your mental health even if you won't regret it. You have to do your research, speak with a counselor, and understand the possible mental and physical risks abortion can bring, even if it's the right choice for you.

Abortions also cost money and recent changes to abortion laws may require you to gain the consent of a parent before getting an abortion. Be sure to check your state and local abortion laws, and go to a certified and legal organization like Planned Parenthood. They can help you find the resources you need to gain access to the right medical care.

As at least one trusted adult should be informed of your pregnancy to provide you with the support you need, you shouldn't make any rash decisions based on their initial reaction. Being told your teenager is pregnant can be quite a shock if you weren't aware they were sexually active.

Counselors can help mediate during this time too. Your parents love you and once they have had time to process this information, they can support you as you make your decision. In the end, the decision is yours and no one else. But pregnancy isn't the only risk you face.

Sexually Transmitted Diseases

Sexually transmitted diseases (STDs) are diseases passed through sexual contact between two individuals, one of which was the carrier of the STD. While you might not display symptoms, the disease can still be harmful to your health and transferable to your sexual partners.

Preventing Sexually Transmitted Diseases

STDs can be transmitted through oral, vaginal, and anal sex and anyone who is sexually active can get an STD. This disease is commonly transferred through skin-to-skin contact and sharing bodily fluids, so the best way to avoid contracting an STD would be to abstain from any type of sex. However, latex condoms that have been used correctly, a mutually monogamous relationship (you and your partner only have sex with each other), and regular STD testing can lower your risk of contracting such a disease.

What to Do if You Get a Sexually Transmitted Disease

The best way to determine if you have an STD is to get tested because not everyone experiences symptoms. Websites such as *GetTested* can help you find an STD testing center nearby; otherwise, you could speak with your healthcare provider. STDs require medical attention.

You cannot avoid treatment as you could unfairly put your partners and your continued health at risk. If you do have an STD, you should avoid having sex while undergoing treatment, and follow-up tests will also be necessary to ensure the treatment has worked.

Most Common Types of Sexually Transmitted Diseases

- **HIV/AIDS**: There is no cure for this virus which has the ability to destroy your body's ability to fight off infections. This makes you more susceptible to life-threatening diseases. Spread through unprotected sex with an infected partner or contact with infected blood and contaminated needles, there are medications to help individuals manage this disease, but it will impact the rest of your life regardless.

- **Human papillomavirus (HPV)**: This disease can cause genital warts inside and outside of your genitals and rectum, but not everyone experiences symptoms. This doesn't mean you haven't been infected or can't pass it on to others. Women who contract HPV are at a higher risk of developing cervical cancer, but regular Pap tests can help your healthcare provider identify any abnormal cancer cells. There is an HPV vaccine, but you should first discuss it with your healthcare provider.

- **Genital herpes**: This STD is caused by the herpes simplex virus (HSV). Symptoms of this disease manifest as a tingling or burning sensation in your genital and rectal area that develops into blisters or open sores that are very painful. These sores might go away with antiviral medicine, which can also reduce your symptoms, but the virus will stay in your body.

- **Hepatitis B**: The hepatitis B virus (HBV) stays in your body to cause long-lasting and long-term liver problems. This STD has a range of symptoms similar to the flu, such as throwing up or feeling nauseous, mild fever, a lack of appetite, fatigue, turning the whites of your eyes yellow, belly pain, and darker urine. Hepatitis B can lead to serious issues like liver cancer and failure, severe illness, permanent scarring of your liver, and death when left untreated.

- **Syphilis**: You will first experience painful, open sores around your vagina which can lead to a short-term rash. When left untreated, syphilis can impact your nervous system and heart.

- **Gonorrhea**: You may experience unusual discharge from your vagina and rectum, as well as painful or difficult bowel movements and urination. Women are often at risk of more serious complications like pelvic inflammatory diseases, infertility, and ectopic pregnancy.

- **Chlamydia**: This STD causes unusual discharge from your vagina and rectum, including bleeding and a burning sensation while urinating. You may not even experience symptoms, but left untreated, chlamydia can cause serious complications such as infertility, pelvic inflammatory disease, and ectopic pregnancy.

- **Pelvic inflammatory disease (PID)**: When your uterus, fallopian tubes, and reproductive organs become infected, causing you to experience belly pain and other serious complications that impact your health.

- **Pubic lice (crabs)**: Spread through skin-to-skin contact, these pinhead-sized insects live in your pubic hair near your genitals, armpit hair, eyebrows, and eyelashes. Lice can cause severe itchiness that gets worse at night and may also cause skin redness and irritation if they bite you.

These are just some of the most common STDs you could contract, but this list and its symptoms are not exhaustive. Regular STD screening, taking the necessary precautions, or even abstaining from any type of sex are some of the ways you can keep yourself safe. It's easy to tell you that you're young and should abstain from sex, but you're also a curious teen capable of making your own decisions. Just make sure your decisions are well-informed and thought through.

When you are born a girl, the world is a lot more dangerous and judgmental towards you than it is for boys. Our society's obsession with sex and using and manipulating women for the benefit of others put you at further risk. You need to learn how to keep yourself physically, mentally, emotionally, and socially safe, especially with the rise in social media's popularity. Chapter 9 will help you better understand the dangers you could face from sexual predators in everyday life.

NOTES TO SELF

Write your thoughts, feelings, comments and anything you need to get off your chest or just make notes. This is your book, your space, take control.

NOTES TO SELF

Write your thoughts, feelings, comments and anything you need to get off your chest or just make notes. This is your book, your space, take control.

Chapter 9:

Let's Talk About Sexual

Predators

We must send a message across the world that there is no disgrace in being a survivor of sexual violence—the shame is on the aggressor. –Angelina Jolie

You should never feel ashamed or guilty if you ever experience, or have experienced, harassment or sexual assault. No woman—regardless of her age, race, sexual orientation, or lifestyle—should ever have to experience abuse of any kind. While women are given more respect and have gained an increase in equality over the years, we still face many challenges and threats to our well-being and safety. Modern society is still doing its best to take advantage of women, especially young teenage girls. You deserve better than the bare minimum of basic decency and respect, but you are also a target of abuse, sexual grooming, and harassment due to your gender. So, what can you do to keep yourself safe?

Please note: The details in this chapter aren't necessarily exhaustive as every state and jurisdiction has varying requirements for each topic discussed here. Please use the information to help you assess the laws of your state or jurisdiction so you can better understand how to protect yourself and what to do should you experience any of the crimes discussed here.

Sexual Grooming

Sexual grooming is when a person, usually an adult, uses specific behaviors and strategies to gain access to a child so they can manipulate them and prepare them for abuse, without being detected by the child's guardians, family members, or friends. Sexual grooming can occur at any age and often takes on a similar methodology. An abuser's aim is to isolate their vulnerable victim until the victim is dependent on the abuser.

Grooming is a process and abusers are calculating, making their end goal easy to miss. Fortunately, understanding what grooming is and being able to identify such behaviors can help you keep yourself safe from people trying to take advantage of you. Sexual and online grooming takes on a similar structure involving five main steps:

- **Victim selection:** Groomers (also called the "perpetrator" and "abuser") are adults in a position of power, including mentors, coaches, teachers, or any individual who is generally older and has connections, power, status, seniority, and wealth that you don't have. They select their victims based on perceived vulnerabilities and how easily they can gain access to them. As such, they often target abuse survivors, people who lack confidence and self-esteem, have intellectual or physical disabilities, are unpopular, spend a lot of time alone, are normally unsupervised, or have family problems. Don't underestimate a groomer. Abusers are calculating and will carefully plan how they will manipulate you.

- **Gaining access:** The abuser will then begin working to physically and emotionally separate you—without anyone noticing—from your guardians, family, and friends. Teenagers are often targeted because it's easier to gain access to them due to their increased independence, lack of adult supervision, and the ease with which they can often manipulate and isolate teens. Remember, the aim of isolating yourself is to prevent you from reaching out for help or being able to run away from the abuser.

- **Developing trust:** Attention, flattery, gifts, and sharing secrets are just some strategies abusers use to gain their victim's trust and make them feel obligated to stay. They may also slander and insult the people you care about, or charm them so no one suspects their true motives. Abusers also make you feel like they are the only person in the world who could understand and love you. This form of manipulation makes you believe you have entered a loving relationship when your abuser is aiming to keep you quiet so they can remain undetected.

- **Desensitization:** After gaining your trust, the abuser will continue to isolate you and start initiating non-sexual touch (like hugs or a hand on the leg). They may also engage in seemingly innocent activities with you, like reading a book or watching a movie. Eventually, these activities start taking a more explicit nature as the abuser begins exposing you to more sexual touches and material, like porn. Victims may find it difficult to say "no" because it makes them feel guilty after agreeing to everything else and accepting the abuser's gifts. The abuse, often sexual abuse, will begin.

- **Maintenance:** Abusers will do everything they can to retain control over their victims. If you try to leave them, they might start out by threatening to harm themselves or start claiming they couldn't sleep or eat because you wouldn't [insert sexual activity]. These statements are false. The abuser is only trying to stay in control. If this strategy doesn't work, they may begin to threaten you or your family with violence if you reach out for help or tell anyone what's really happening. These threats and further acts of violence against the victim may cause them to feel like the abuse is their fault, preventing them from seeking help and reporting the abuse. But abuse of any kind will **NEVER** be your fault! The perpetrator will always be the only one to blame.

Online Predators

As society has begun to socialize in online spaces to connect with people from all over the world, grooming has grown and adapted to fit the virtual world. Online predators work in a similar fashion to sexual groomers, except they have adapted their tactics to an online space. In the worst-case scenario, these predators convince their victims to meet them in person so they can gain physical control over the victim.

The rise in social media's popularity, and everyone's tendency to share nearly all of their personal information online, has made the internet a dangerous place for girls. While you can meet kind, genuine people on the internet and make friends, it's very easy for sexual predators to use a fake username, stolen profile photo, and other fake information to create a persona specifically for their chosen victim.

Online predators also start by gaining your trust through compliments, pretending to share your interests and gifts, and creating an online relationship. Once they've gained your trust and established this relationship, they will start steering the conversation to more sexual and personal topics. They may even begin sending you explicit pictures and videos, or requesting that you send them explicit videos and images of yourself. If you try to end this relationship, they may resort to blackmailing you by threatening to expose the images and messages to your family, friends, or the internet. This prevents many young girls from seeking help.

While online predators can be difficult to detect, they share many similarities with regular sexual groomers. They will ask you to keep your relationship a secret, manipulate you, and do their best to gain your trust. Knowledge will be crucial in helping you identify these behaviors so you can keep yourself safe from online predators. As a teenager, you might want many social media followers, so you switch off your privacy settings. This can put you at an increased risk of sexual predators as they can view your profile and personal information, follow, and message you without any extra security stopping them. Turn your privacy settings on and carefully consider the people requesting to follow you, as well as the people you want to follow.

This may seem paranoid and dramatic, but the rise of violence against women in online and real-life environments mean that safety and guarding yourself is your number one priority, especially as a young girl. Some tips for keeping yourself safe include:

- avoiding suggestive usernames or photos on your social media accounts.

- ending a conversation, blocking, reporting, and deleting accounts of any person who tries to start a personal or sexual conversation with you, this includes inappropriate comments or conversations that make you uncomfortable.

- NEVER arranging to meet online people in real life.

- NEVER giving away any personal information or details a person can use to figure out where you live, go to school, work, or shop.

If you ever feel like the person you're talking to online isn't who they appear to be; has requested or sent you explicit messages, videos, or images; or has made you feel uncomfortable, tell a trusted adult without telling the person you suspect. Save the messages the online individual sent you, using screenshots, so you have evidence that can be used when reporting the suspected predator to your local police or tiplines like *CyberTipline* at www.cybertipline.com.

The National Center for Missing and Exploited Children can also help you, or you could call (800) 843-5678 to report the inappropriate and explicit messages, content, or behavior of the suspected predator *(Staying safe from online predators*, n.d.: par. 15-16).

Sexual Assault

Sexual assault is any activity that includes the unwanted and forced contact of one person's body parts (like the breasts, buttocks, or genitals) with the body parts of the person forcing the contact (called the "perpetrator," "abuser," or "rapist"). Sexual assault covers a broad category of unwanted and forced sexual activities, including rape. These activities are all illegal and you have the right to report these activities, the perpetrators, and pursue legal action if you ever experience any of them.

You already know that when you have consented to a sexual activity, you have freely decided to engage in that activity; however, coercion (a type of sexual assault) occurs when you are pressured or forced into such activities because you feel as though you don't have a choice, can't say "no" (or struggle to say "no" for fear of your physical safety), were overpowered by the other person, or drugged. Sexual assault is also the phrase used to refer to forced sexual activities committed by a perpetrator from outside your family, while sexual abuse occurs when a family member commits the abuse.

Rape

Rape is about power, not sex. This term includes any penetration of your vagina or anus, no matter how minor, by another person's body part or an object. This term includes the oral penetration by a sex organ of another person. All these activities have a few things in common: They are unwanted actions you did not consent to, were pressured or forced into, or the perpetrator took away your ability to fight back using violence, strength, or drugs (*Rape*, 2015: par. 1-2). Regardless of whether the perpetrator is a stranger, acquaintance, partner, friend, or family member, any action falling under these conditions is considered rape.

While rape is accompanied by feelings of shame and guilt, these emotions are weaponized by perpetrators so they can get away with their crimes and force you to take the blame when you are NOT at fault. Regardless of what you wore, said, acted, or did, you never deserve to be raped or abused in this way. No one has the right to have sex of any sort with you against your will. The blame lies only with the rapist.

There are a few precautions you can take to keep yourself safe as you live your life, but these tips aren't exhaustive. First, expect respect from others and keep your standards high. Don't settle for anything less because you deserve more than the bare minimum of basic respect and kindness from other people. Don't allow other people to touch you without your permission, even if this means making a big, dramatic scene. This can actually scare off potential perpetrators if they want to remain undetected, even if they are being bold.

Trust your instincts, speak your mind, and act immediately. Also, have an exit and safety plan that your caregivers and friends are all familiar with. This can keep you and your friends safe and decrease your risk of abuse. While out with friends or by yourself, keep a close eye on your drinks, and don't let others pour them or hold them for you.

You shouldn't accept drinks from anyone either, even if they are closed, because drinks are the easiest way for perpetrators to drug you. Some women have been drugged after watching their drink the entire time because of how careful some perpetrators are so always be wary.

If It Happens, What Do You Do?

After a rape or sexual assault has occurred, you have to seek immediate medical care without cleaning up, changing your clothes, showering, douching, or washing any part of your body, not even your hands. This can be a difficult instinct to fight, but during a medical examination, a specialist can use your clothing and body to collect evidence of the perpetrator's crime so if you do decide to press charges or report the crime, you have the medical exam and evidence to support you.

A friend or trusted adult can accompany you to provide you with support during this time. However, if you don't want anyone to know, your local rape crisis center can provide you with an advocate who will stay by your side throughout the examination and reporting process.

While you can see a healthcare provider a few days after the crime, you do have to seek medical attention because rape can cause physical, psychological, and emotional injuries that need the correct care and treatment so you can move on, regain your power, and start healing. The perpetrator doesn't get to keep their power over you.

What Happens During the Medical Exam?

A trained counselor or social worker will listen as you recount what happened during the incident. They can help you calm down and feel safe again, and they help you better understand what will happen during the medical exam as different states and jurisdictions have different requirements. In general, you will undergo STD and HIV/AIDS tests so you can be effectively treated as soon as possible.

As a woman, you can also request to be treated for unwanted pregnancy. An internal examination can check for internal injuries so they can be effectively treated as well. Samples of the rapist's hair, body fluids, nails, or skin will be collected by a trained technician from your clothes and body.

If you think you may have been drugged, a toxicology test can be requested. During the medical examination, you have the power—at any stage—to ask them to stop or not conduct a test as the procedures have been designed in a way to help you gain control after such a traumatic experience (*Rape*, 2015: par. 23-31).

Your Mental Health

Your mental health will also be greatly affected by such a traumatic event. Professional help, either in one-on-one or group settings, can help you work through your pain and trauma so you can start regaining your power, control, and life. Rape triggers a number of emotions: anger guilt, shame, confusion, etc. You should **never** feel ashamed or guilty about what happened. It was not your fault, and it will never be your fault.

Female Genital Mutilation

Any procedure or injury to the female genitalia or organs for non-medical reasons is known as "female genital mutilation" (FGM) (World Health Organization, 2023: par. 1). This procedure has no medical benefits and can cause a number of serious health issues and complications like severe bleeding, problematic menstrual cycles, painful sex and childbirth, issues urinating, infections, and an increased risk of death in women, mothers, and babies. FGM is considered a violation of a woman's and girl's human rights.

Types of Female Genital Mutilation

- **Type 1:** Partial or total removal of the external and visible part of the clitoris and fold of skin surrounding this organ.

- **Type 2:** Partial or total removal of the clitoral glans and inner folds of the vulva, with or without the removal of the external folds of skin.

- **Type 3:** Creating a covering seal to narrow the vaginal opening, called "infibulation."

- **Type 4:** Any and all other harmful procedures to the female genitalia for non-medical reasons (World Health Organization, 2023: par. 10-15).

Cultural Factors

FGM is classified as a social convention that is supposed to prepare young girls for adulthood and marriage by exerting control over her virginity and fidelity before and after marriage. In certain cultures, FGM is considered a necessary part of raising a girl (World Health Organization, 2023: par. 39-43).

Who Is at Risk?

Girls aged between infancy and adolescence—and sometimes adult women—are subjected to FGM. This practice mainly occurs in the eastern, north-eastern, and western regions of Africa, and some of the countries in Asia and the Middle East (World Health Organization, 2023: par. 38).

As a young girl, the world poses many dangers to your continued health and well-being. Growing up can be extremely stressful as you do your best to keep yourself safe while navigating puberty and threats to your safety.

Knowledge will become a valuable tool in helping you identify and stop potential problems before they happen or progress. To be able to do this, you also need to understand what the laws surrounding sex, relationships, and abortions are. Chapter 10 will briefly discuss some of the general laws surrounding these topics, so you have a starting point for checking the laws of your state or jurisdiction.

NOTES TO SELF

Write your thoughts, feelings, comments and anything you need to get off your chest or just make notes. This is your book, your space, take control.

NOTES TO SELF

Write your thoughts, feelings, comments and anything you need to get off your chest or just make notes. This is your book, your space, take control.

Chapter 10:

Let's Talk About the Laws

I have chosen to no longer be apologetic for my femaleness and my femininity. And I want to be respected in all of my femaleness because I deserve to be. –Chimamanda Ngozi Adichie

While there are a number of laws that remain the same for every state in the United States, like murder being illegal, certain laws—such as those surrounding the age of consent, rape, abortion, and relationships—have minor variations that could result in you or your partner breaking the law. I will discuss some of these laws here, but I recommend that you do your own research to check how these laws are applicable to your state, how they differ, and how this could affect you at different ages.

As you move through adolescence, you have to practice taking responsibility. This is one of the first steps you can take to practice this skill. Even if you aren't currently in a relationship or having sex, understanding how the law of your state can protect you will be important throughout your life, especially as a girl.

Laws for Consent

The laws relating to consent differ between states, meaning a person could be convicted of statutory rape even though both partners consented. But what does this mean? *Statutory rape* is a crime that occurs when two parties take part in sexual activities (of any kind) that would be legal if not for the age of at least one partner (ASPE, 2004: par. 25).

This age is based on the age of consent specific to that state. The legal *age of consent* differs between states, but it generally ranges between 16, 17, and 18 years old in the United States. However, two additional age groups also need to be considered. Being *below the age of consent* means you cannot legally consent to sexual intercourse of any kind, regardless of the circumstances. However, if you are above the minimum age of consent, but still below the age of consent, the law needs to consider the difference in age between you and your partner, where you have both agreed and consented to sexual intercourse, before prosecuting.

Additionally, the law also has to consider your partner's age as the *minimum age of a defender for prosecution* is the age below which a person can be prosecuted for engaging in sexual activities with a minor; however, this law will only apply when the youngest partner is above a certain age (ASPE, 2004: par. 59-63). Becoming aware of these laws will be important as soon as you feel ready to start dating, but especially when you feel ready to have sex. Ensure you understand how the laws regarding age and consent work in your state, as well as how they will apply to you and your partner.

Laws on Relationships

There are no laws relating specifically to dating and age; however, depending on your state's legal age of consent and the ages of you and your partner, statutory rape laws could apply. This means that even if both partners are aware of their ages and have agreed to the romantic relationship, the older partner is at risk of being prosecuted for statutory rape if the youngest partner is below the age of consent. However, these laws also differ depending on this age difference. While such laws may seem unfair to you when you are in a happy relationship, they have been created to prevent individuals who are older than you, especially those in positions of power, from taking advantage of you and abusing you for their own gain.

Even though there are no laws specifically related to dating, there are laws that prevent an older individual from marrying a child under the age of consent. In most states, the minimum age for marriage is 18 years old (Levey, 2021: par. 4).

While many states do, unfortunately, allows special provisions that could allow individuals under the age of consent to marry, UNICEF has been working to make the minimum age for marriage 18 years old due to the harm that getting married at a young age can result in. This may sound unfair, but many of the girls marrying under the age of consent are being forced into these marriages for various reasons, including poverty or their new spouse taking advantage of their family's misfortunes. In other words, these young girls often have no choice in their marriage, putting them at an increased risk of harm. UNICEF has reported that when girls under 18 years old get married, they are put at a higher risk of abuse by their spouse, death (especially after the birth of their first child, which also puts their baby at risk), higher rates of divorce, and getting stuck in the cycle of poverty (Ferguson, 2018: par. 8-10).

Your parents' rules and the laws surrounding sex and marriage may seem unfair to you, when you think you are in a happy, loving relationship. While some teens do have successful relationships that last well into their adult years, resulting in long and happy marriages, even more teens—especially girls—are physically and sexually abused by older men and men in positions of power. If your partner truly cares about and loves you, they won't mind waiting until you are ready and above the legal age of consent before either of you engage in any activities that could potentially alter your future, such as marriage and sex.

Laws on Abortions

Roe v. Wade is a Supreme Court ruling that took place in the United States in 1973 that established abortion as a fundamental human right (*After Roe fell: Abortion laws by state*, n.d.: par. 52). In June 2022, this ruling was overturned, putting the reproductive rights of any individual who has the ability to fall pregnant and have a baby at risk.

States now have the legal ability to choose to purposefully make abortion illegal. Essentially, they have increased control over the reproductive rights of people with uteruses. *The Center for Reproductive Rights* can help you better understand how this ruling could affect you as the law, restrictions, and exceptions are constantly changing state-to-state.

There has been major confusion among doctors, abortion clinics, and patients in regard to the legality of abortion and abortion care. This constant shift between legal and illegal, or only legal under certain circumstances, has also caused a number of other issues that put the health and safety of patients seeking abortion care at risk. Laws surrounding abortion continue to change well into 2023 (Nash and Ephross, 2022).

Please stay up-to-date on how these changes affect the abortion laws of your state. Regardless of your stance on abortion or whether you will ever need to seek abortion care, abortion has saved the lives of many individuals with uteruses. Without appropriate care, pregnant individuals who are desperate may resort to illegal and unsafe methods of abortion that often result in their death or serious injury. Should you ever need to seek abortion care, please seek the help of a certified and legal abortion clinic and keep your knowledge up-to-date.

10 Strange Laws in the United States

The law has always been intricate and complicated. There's a reason why lawyers study for so long and get paid so much. But there are also a number of laws that haven't changed for many, many years because they were forgotten when they were no longer needed. Although, some of these laws also came about because of unique circumstances. While I can't detail how some of these strange laws came about, the list that follows includes 10 of some of the strangest laws found in the U.S. (Dunnell, 2021).

- In North Carolina, it's illegal to cohabitate with a partner if you're not married.

- In Michigan, it's illegal to seduce unmarried women.

- You're not allowed to sell "boobie pillows" (stuffed objects depicting female breasts) in Kern County, California.

- In Utah, you can legally marry your first cousin if you're over the age of 55.

- If either partner has an STD, you're not allowed to legally get married in Nebraska.

- 18 states have laws against adultery.

- It's illegal to flirt in New Jersey.

- In South Carolina, it's a crime not to follow through on a promise to marry someone.

- You're not allowed to own more than six dildos in Texas.

- In Mississippi, it's illegal to explain to someone what polygamy is.

This chapter barely scratches the surface of the laws relating to consent, rape, marriage, and abortion due to the detail and exceptions each law contains. And that's without taking into account the way each law differs in every state. However, you now have the knowledge you need to build a foundation for not only protecting yourself, but also preventing other people from taking advantage of you.

You are growing up and gaining control over your life and your body. It's **your** right to decide what to do with it, as long as you aren't endangering yourself or taking part in activities that could harm you in the future. That's also why the law has created certain safeguards, like the age of consent. Stay up-to-date, always gather new knowledge, and work with your friends and family to stay safe throughout your teenage years.

NOTES TO SELF

Write your thoughts, feelings, comments and anything you need to get off your chest or just make notes. This is your book, your space, take control.

NOTES TO SELF

Write your thoughts, feelings, comments and anything you need to get off your chest or just make notes. This is your book, your space, take control.

Conclusion

A girl should be two things: who and what she wants. –Coco
Chanel

You may be feeling overwhelmed with all the new information that going through adolescence brings. Take a moment to close your eyes and breathe. You can always go back and reread the chapters as you go through each stage of puberty. Puberty can be very scary, but you aren't alone. You are now armed with the knowledge you need to better understand the changes you're going through, as well as how they will affect your life and relationships. But just because you finished this book doesn't mean your work is done.

You have to take what you learned and apply it in your everyday life and social situations. Adolescence is a time of constant change and learning. Keep building your knowledge base, learn from your mistakes, ask questions and be curious, but also remain cautious. Everything you have learned from this book can be adapted to suit your needs and lifestyle as they change throughout adolescence. So be sure to take what you have learned and make it work for you.

The fluctuating hormones that accompany puberty can make this time of your life seem more confusing and stressful than it has to be. It's critical that you learn how to take care of yourself properly because this is a skill you will continue practicing as an adult.

Your physical, mental, and emotional well-being will always need to be taken care of, and proper care can help you continue living a healthy and happy life. Understanding how the changes that accompany puberty can affect you can help you improve your health, while also learning to accept your body as it is despite the changes you are going through.

There are multiple stages to puberty and the rate at which you move through them will differ from your friends. That's normal and expected. While you have reached a stage in your life where you don't want to stick out, but also want to keep up with your friends, you need to remember that your puberty will be unique to you.

Don't try to rush or force things. Understanding how puberty will affect you helps you prepare so you can deal with these changes in a way that won't stress you out even more or disrupt your life. So, remember to stock up your vanity cabinet and school bag just in case your period tries to sneak up on you.

Adolescence is a big change in your life. These changes disrupt your routines, relationships, and daily life, but this disruption isn't necessarily bad. It gives you the opportunity to create new healthy habits that can help you manage adolescence in a way that won't negatively impact your future. Understanding how peer pressure and substances like alcohol, drugs, and cigarettes can affect you are all an important part of creating healthy habits.

No one can stop you from being curious about these substances or perhaps experimenting with them against the advice of your guardians, but you have to understand the risks involved so you can take responsibility and practice basic safety. Remember that one moment of impulsivity can trigger a chain reaction of events that can change the course of your life. Thinking things through, finding balance, and taking time to think things through is critical to surviving adolescence in one piece.

This is especially important for your relationships. Unfortunately, all the relationships in your life will experience changes. It's easy to get into arguments with your guardians. You may be panicking about the changes that adolescence brings, but your guardians are also panicking. You are gaining more responsibility and independence as you grow up. This loss of control over your life by your guardians can be particularly scary considering the world we currently live in.

Guardians might fight to regain control over your life, but if you both take time to calm down before discussing concerns, rules, and consequences, you can both work on resolving problems in a way that benefits both parties. This takes conscious effort, but it's worth it.

Healthy relationships with family, friends, and romantic partners are critical to your emotional, mental, and physical well-being, but it also takes effort from both parties. Don't feel guilty about doing what is best for you if the other person isn't trying to make an effort even after you have put the work in.

Navigating relationships is only the first step because you may also start dating during adolescence. Dating at any age is nerve-wracking and awkward, especially when you care about the other person. If anything, nerves are a good sign because it shows that neither party wants to mess the date up.

Dating in real life is nothing like the movies, but you can create a game plan to help keep you safe, reduce your nerves, and enjoy your first date despite the anxiety.

This of course leads to curiosity about sex. The world and the media are always making such a big deal about it that it's hard not to be curious, especially when you have hormones flowing through your body. The best way for you to learn to resist peer pressure, keep yourself safe, and make the decision to have sex when you are ready is to understand what sex involves, including the different types of sex and how you can practice safe sex. Remember, deciding to have sex will always be your decision because it's your body.

That's why you have to understand the importance of consent. You will always have the right to say "no" at any stage, regardless of the circumstances, without feeling guilty about it. Consent is also key for enforcing your sexual boundaries so other people can't take advantage of you. If anyone tries to pressure or physically force you into having sex with them, you have to remember that it will never be your fault.

Consent is also important because sex is accompanied by a number of risks, pregnancy and STDs being the two main ones. Understanding how these two factors can be risky and how they impact your life and health can help you determine the best way to keep yourself safe, even if that means you decide to abstain from sex until marriage.

There is no shame in abstinence, just like there is no shame in deciding to practice safe sex before marriage. The decision will only ever be yours, but ensure you have all the facts before making this decision.

But these aren't the only risks you face. Being a girl and entering adolescence means your exposure to potential sexual predators increases. Your safety and well-being are threatened in an online and physical space. These predators can be calculating and manipulative, but if you stay up-to-date on the potential tactics and strategies they use, you can learn to identify the red flags and keep yourself safe. Even if you don't notice any red flags, always trust your gut instincts.

If you ever feel uncomfortable or a situation seems wrong, be safe and get out of there as soon as you can. You are never to blame for the crimes committed against you. The blame lies only with the perpetrator.

Keeping yourself safe also means understanding the rules. Certain laws have been put in place to prevent those who are older than you—even by a few years— and who are in positions of power and authority from taking advantage of your age and status. These laws differ in different states.

While I briefly discussed them, you have to do your own research to better understand the legal risks of engaging in sex when you are under the age of consent, even if the sex is consensual. This also means understanding which laws protect you, and how, so you can keep yourself safe and seek justice should it ever come to that.

Puberty may be scary, but living your life the way you want to, despite the changes puberty brings, is brave. As you move through adolescence, you need to learn how to accept responsibility for your body and your decisions. This book has provided you with the tools, strategies, and information you need to help you make the right decisions and keep yourself safe. It's time you take what you have learned and use it to help you navigate adolescence and your relationships.

If you have enjoyed the content of this book and think it can help other teenage girls as well, please leave a review on Amazon and help me change the lives of other girls.

NOTES TO SELF

Write your thoughts, feelings, comments and anything you need to get off your chest or just make notes. This is your book, your space, take control.

NOTES TO SELF

Write your thoughts, feelings, comments and anything you need to get off your chest or just make notes. This is your book, your space, take control.

References

After Roe fell: Abortion laws by state. (n.d.). Center for Reproductive Rights. https://reproductiverights.org/maps/abortion-laws-by-state/

All about sex. (n.d.). Planned Parenthood. https://www.plannedparenthood.org/learn/teens/sex/all-about-sex

All about sunscreen. (2022, July). The Skin Cancer Foundation. https://www.skincancer.org/skin-cancer-prevention/sun-protection/sunscreen/

Allen, B., and Miller, K. (2019, April 6). *Physical development in girls: What to expect during puberty.* HealthyChildren.org. https://www.healthychildren.org/English/ages-stages/gradeschool/puberty/Pages/Physical-Development-Girls-What-to-Expect.aspx

Andrew Smith quote: "Expired condoms are like nuclear waste: there's nothing sensible you can do with it." (n.d.). Quotefancy.com. https://quotefancy.com/quote/2189671/Andrew-Smith-Expired-condoms-are-like-nuclear-waste-there-s-nothing-sensible-you-can-do

ASPE. (2004, December 14). *Statutory rape: A guide to state laws and reporting requirements.* ASPE Office of the Assistant Secretary for Planning and Evaluation. https://aspe.hhs.gov/reports/statutory-rape-guide-state-laws-reporting-requirements-1

Barghouty, L. (2019, October 31). *For women, lung illness is only the first toll of vaping.* Bustle. https://www.bustle.com/p/how-will-vaping-affect-women-19282665

Benveniste, A. (2022, December 14). First-time sex: 20 Questions about losing your virginity, answered. *Teen Vogue.* https://www.teenvogue.com/story/20-questions-about-your-first-time-have-sex-answered

Berg, M. (2022, April 15). Sexual boundaries: How to set them. *Planned Parenthood Federation of America.* https://www.plannedparenthood.org/blog/how-to-set-sexual-boundaries

Birth control methods. (2022, December 29). OASH Office on Women's Health. https://www.womenshealth.gov/a-z-topics/birth-control-methods

Body image: pre-teens and teenagers. (2022, September 12). Raising Children Network. https://raisingchildren.net.au/pre-teens/healthy-lifestyle/body-image/body-image-teens

Bridges, F. (2022, October 12). 10 Ways to build confidence. *Forbes.*

https://www.forbes.com/sites/francesbridges/
2017/07/21/10-ways-to-build-
confidence/?sh=5fa1304b3c59

Buffum Taylor, R. (2022, August 8). *Teenage pregnancy.*
WebMD.
https://www.webmd.com/baby/teen-
pregnancy-medical-risks-and-realities

CDC. (n.d.). *Get Tested: National HIV, STD, and Hepatitis Testing.* Centers for Disease Control and Prevention. https://gettested.cdc.gov/

CDC. (2014). *Smoking and youth.* In Centers for Disease Control and Prevention. https://www.cdc.gov/tobacco/data_statistics/s gr/50th- anniversary/pdfs/fs_smoking_youth_508.pdf

CDC. (2022a, April 12). *CDC fact sheet: Information for teens and young adults: Staying healthy and preventing STDs.* Centers for Disease Control and Prevention. https://www.cdc.gov/std/life- stages-populations/stdfact-teens.htm

CDC. (2022b, October 26). *Underage Drinking.* Centers for Disease Control and Prevention. https://www.cdc.gov/alcohol/fact- sheets/underage-drinking.htm

"Change is inevitable, growth is optional" quote. (2021, February 28) Motivationalspeaks. https://motivationalspeaks.com/change-is- inevitable/

Cherry, K. (2022a, October 6). *10 Ways to build resilience.* Verywell Mind. https://www.verywellmind.com/ways-to-become-more-resilient-2795063

Cherry, K. (2022b, November 7). *What is emotional intelligence? The ability to perceive, evaluate, express, and control emotions.* Verywell Mind. https://www.verywellmind.com/what-is-emotional-intelligence-2795423

Contact us. (n.d.). Center for Reproductive Rights. https://reproductiverights.org/about-us/contact-us/

Dunnell, T. (2021, February 8). *10 Strange sex laws in the United States.* Mental Floss. https://www.mentalfloss.com/article/641817/strange-sex-laws-united-states

E-cigarettes and teens. (2020, February). The Royal Children's Hospital Melbourne. https://www.rch.org.au/kidsinfo/fact_sheets/E-cigarettes_and_teens/

Ehmke, R. (2023, February 2). Teens and romantic relationships. *Child Mind Institute.* https://childmind.org/article/how-to-help-kids-have-good-romantic-relationships/

11 Facts about teen pregnancy. (2015). DoSomething.org. https://www.dosomething.org/us/facts/11-facts-about-teen-pregnancy

Elsesser, K. (2021, October 5). Here's how Instagram harms young women according to research. *Forbes.* https://www.forbes.com/sites/kimelsesser/2021/10/05/heres-how-instagram-harms-young-women-according-to-research/?sh=18b28032255a

Everything you wanted to know about puberty. (n.d.). Nemours Teens Health. https://kidshealth.org/en/teens/puberty.html

Family Health Team. (2019, June 12). *Can eating too many carrots turn your skin orange?* Cleveland Clinic. https://health.clevelandclinic.org/can-eating-too-many-carrots-turn-your-skin-orange/

Female reproductive system. (2019, June). Nemours Teens Health. https://kidshealth.org/en/teens/female-repro.html

Ferguson, S. (2018, October 29). *What you need to know about child marriage in the* U.S. UNICEF USA. https://www.unicefusa.org/stories/what-you-need-know-about-child-marriage-us/35059

First date advice: 10 dos and don'ts everybody should know. (2017, June 16). StyleCaster. https://stylecaster.com/first-date-advice/

For teens: *How to make healthy decisions about sex.* (2015, August 1). HealthyChildren.org. https://www.healthychildren.org/English/ages

-stages/teen/dating-sex/Pages/Making-Healthy-Decisions-About-Sex.aspx

Foster, B. (n.d.). *6 Signs your teen is in a toxic relationship.* All Pro Dad. https://www.allprodad.com/6-signs-your-teen-is-in-a-toxic-relationship/

Friends and friendships: Pre-teens and teenagers. (2021, September 13). Raising Children Network. https://raisingchildren.net.au/pre-teens/behaviour/peers-friends-trends/teen-friendships

Getting and giving sexual consent: talking with teenagers. (2023, February 10). Raising Children Network. https://raisingchildren.net.au/teens/communicating-relationships/tough-topics/getting-giving-sexual-consent-talking-with-teens

Gillespie, C. (2018, November 18). *Laws on Underage Dating.* Legal Beagle. https://legalbeagle.com/6503644-ohio-laws-minor-dating-adult.html

Gordon, S. (2021, September 22). *12 Truths about friendship every girl needs to know: Debunking the myths surrounding bully-proof friendships.* Verywell Family. https://www.verywellfamily.com/girls-friendships-and-bullying-4065064

Happiness and wellbeing for pre-teens and teenagers. (2022, October 20). Raising Children Network. https://raisingchildren.net.au/teens/mental-health-physical-health/about-mental-health/happy-teens

#BREAKFREE from shame: Celebrity quotes about sexual assault. (2016, January 8). Marie Claire UK. https://www.marieclaire.co.uk/life/celebrity-quotes-on-sexual-assault-and-rape-22265

Healthy parent-teen relationships. (2018, November 24). The Whole Child. https://www.thewholechild.org/parent-resources/age-13-18/parenting-tips-age-13-18/healthy-parent-teen-relationships/

HealthyPlace Staff Writer. (2022, March 21). *For teens: Are you really ready for sex?* HealthyPlace. https://www.healthyplace.com/relationships/teen-relationships/for-teens-are-you-really-ready-for-sex

Helping teens resist sexual pressure. (2009, February 11). HealthyChildren.org. https://www.healthychildren.org/English/ages-stages/teen/dating-sex/Pages/Helping-Teens-Resist-Sexual-Pressure.aspx

Hepatitis B. (2020, February). Nemours Teens Health. https://kidshealth.org/en/teens/std-hepatitis.html

How to find the right bra. (2015, November 6). Teen Help. https://www.teenhelp.com/puberty/how-to-find-the-right-bra/

How to Handle Peer Pressure. (2022, February). Nemours Kids Health. https://kidshealth.org/en/kids/peer-pressure.html

Intimate hygiene for teen girls and females. (n.d.). CAREFREE® Pantyliners. https://www.carefreearabia.com/en/intimate-teen-hygiene

Isabelle, K. (n.d.). *Katharine Isabelle Quote.* A-Z Quotes. https://www.azquotes.com/quote/1191209

Jacobson, R. (2022, June 14). How to talk to kids about sex and consent. *Child Mind Institute.* https://childmind.org/article/how-talk-kids-sex-consent-boundaries/

Jegllc, E. L. (2020, February 5). But they went willingly—Understanding teen sexual grooming. *Psychology Today.* https://www.psychologytoday.com/us/blog/protecting-children-sexual-abuse/202002/they-went-willingly-understanding-teen-sexual-grooming

Jeurgens, J., and Hampton, D. (2023, January 19). *Health effects of teen substance abuse.* Addiction Center. https://www.addictioncenter.com/teenage-drug-abuse/health-effects-teen-substance-abuse/

Johansson, S. (n.d.). *Scarlett Johansson quote.* A-Z Quotes. https://www.azquotes.com/quote/1104861

Kirby, S. (2023, January 26). *Sex quotes for relationships, love and intimacy.* Everyday Power. https://everydaypower.com/sex-quotes/

Kraut, M. E. (n.d.). *Children and grooming/Online predators.* Child Crime Prevention & Safety Center. https://childsafety.losangelescriminallawyer.pro /children-and-grooming-online-predators.html

Langlois, C. (2011, November 4). *Siblings entering the teenage years.* Canadian Living. https://www.canadianliving.com/life-and-relationships/family/article/siblings-entering-the-teenage-years

Leonard, J. (2018, April 24). What essential oils are good for preventing stretch marks? *Medical News Today.* https://www.medicalnewstoday.com/articles/3 21595

Levey, J. (2021, September 16). *How old do you have to be to get married in each state?* American Marriage Ministries. https://theamm.org/articles/920-how-old-do-you-have-to-be-to-get-married-in-each-state

Love, G. (2021). *Sex while camping is in tents: Love me ten times.* Goodreads. https://www.goodreads.com/work/quotes/93 030904-sex-while-camping-is-in-tents-love-me-ten-times

Male reproductive system. (2019, July). Nemours Kids Health. https://kidshealth.org/en/teens/male-repro.html

Managing the effects of social media on teen girls. (2020, March 11). Northwestern: The Family Institute.

https://counseling.northwestern.edu/blog/effe cts-social-media-teen-girls/

Mayo Clinic Staff. (2022, October 4). *Teen drug abuse: Help your teen avoid drugs.* Mayo Clinic. https://www.mayoclinic.org/healthy-lifestyle/tween-and-teen-health/in-depth/teen-drug-abuse/art-20045921

Mental health in pre-teens and teenagers. (2022, October 20). Raising Children Network. https://raisingchildren.net.au/pre-teens/mental-health-physical-health/about-mental-health/teen-mental-health

Moods: Helping pre-teens and teens manage emotional ups and downs. (2022, October 20). Raising Children Network. https://raisingchildren.net.au/pre-teens/mental-health-physical-health/about-mental-health/ups-downs

Moore, C. (2019, June 2). *How to practice self-compassion: 8 techniques and tips.* Positive Psychology. https://positivepsychology.com/how-to-practice-self-compassion/

Morin, A. (2022a, July 22). *7 Signs that your teen's romantic relationship is unhealthy.* Verywell Family. https://www.verywellfamily.com/unhealthy-relationship-signs-in-teens-4065362

Morin, A. (2022b, November 29). *12 Truths about teens and dating.* Verywell Family. https://www.verywellfamily.com/five-truths-teens-and-dating-2611146

Nash, E., and Ephross, P. (2022). *State policy trends 2022: In a devastating year, US Supreme Court's decision to overturn Roe leads to bans, confusion and chaos.* Guttmacher Institute. https://doi.org/10.1363/2022.300251

National Child Traumatic Stress Network. (2023). *Teen sexual assault: Information for teens.* https://www.nctsn.org/sites/default/files/reso urces/teen_sexual_assault_teens.pdf

OASH. (2021). *Trends in teen pregnancy and childbearing.* HHS Office of Population Affairs. https://opa.hhs.gov/adolescent-health/reproductive-health-and-teen-pregnancy/trends-teen-pregnancy-and-childbearing

Partnership Staff. (2017, February). *Top 8 Reasons Teens Try Alcohol and Drugs.* Partnership to End Addiction. https://drugfree.org/article/top-8-reasons-teens-try-alcohol-drugs/

Peer Pressure. (n.d.). Nemours Teens Health. https://kidshealth.org/en/teens/peer-pressure.html

Peer pressure or influence: pre-teens and teenagers. (2021, November 3). Raising Children Network. https://raisingchildren.net.au/teens/behaviour /peers-friends-trends/peer-influence

Perry, T. (2022, February 28). *It's getting harder to deny the damage that social media is doing to teenage girls.* Upworthy. https://www.upworthy.com/its-getting-harder-to-deny-the-damage-that-social-media-is-doing-to-teenage-girls

Puberty for girls. (2021, April). Health Direct. https://www.healthdirect.gov.au/puberty-for-girls

Puberty: Stages for boys and girls. (2021, May 12). *Cleveland Clinic.* https://my.clevelandclinic.org/health/articles/22192-puberty

Pubic lice (crabs). (2022, January). Nemours Teens Health. https://kidshealth.org/en/teens/std-lice.html

Rape. (2015, August). Nemours Teens Health. https://kidshealth.org/en/teens/rape-what-to-do.html

Relationships and romance: Pre-teens and teenagers. (2023, February 10). Raising Children Network. https://raisingchildren.net.au/pre-teens/communicating-relationships/romantic-relationships/teen-relationships

Relationships with parents and families: pre-teens and teenagers. (2021, November 29). Raising Children Network. https://raisingchildren.net.au/pre-teens/communicating-relationships/family-relationships/relationships-with-parents-teens

Roberts, T. (n.d.). *Tanya Roberts quotes.* BrainyQuote. https://www.brainyquote.com/authors/tanya-roberts-quotes

Rosen, P. (2022, August 23). *I'm a nonbinary teen: Here's what parents need to know.* Parents. https://www.parents.com/parenting/better-parenting/teenagers/teen-talk/im-a-teen-who-is-nonbinary-heres-what-i-wish-parents-would-know-about-gender/

Sagar, M. (2023, February 10). *The skin: How many skincare products should teens use?* Peaches and Blush. https://peachesandblush.com/the-skin-how-many-skincare-products-should-teens-use/

Sexual orientation and gender identity. (n.d.). Youth.gov. https://youth.gov/youth-topics/lgbt

Sexually transmitted infections in teens. (n.d.). Stanford Medicine Children's Health. https://www.stanfordchildrens.org/en/topic/default?id=sexually-transmitted-diseases-in-adolescents-90-P01654

Sibling fighting: Pre-teens and teenagers. (2021, November 3). Raising Children Network. https://raisingchildren.net.au/pre-teens/behaviour/sibling-fights/sibling-fighting

6 Stages of grooming adults and teens: Spotting the red flags. (2020, November 17). *Skills Platform Blog.* https://www.skillsplatform.org/blog/6-stages-of-grooming-adults-and-teens-spotting-the-red-flags/

60 Inspirational quotes for young women. (n.d.). Live Bold and Bloom.

https://liveboldandbloom.com/11/quotes/you
ng-women-inspirational-quotes

Staying safe from online predators. (n.d.). GCFGlobal.
https://edu.gcfglobal.org/en/internetsafetyfork
ids/staying-safe-from-online-predators/1/

Tampons, pads, and other period supplies. (2019, October).
Nemours Teens Health.
https://kidshealth.org/en/teens/supplies.html

Team LovePanky. (n.d.). 60 Secrets to make a woman
orgasm and master the art of making a girl cum
hard. LovePanky.
https://www.lovepanky.com/sensual-
tease/passion-pill/how-to-make-a-woman-
orgasm

Teens: Relationship development. (2019). Stanford Medicine
Children's Health.
https://www.stanfordchildrens.org/en/topic/d
efault?id=relationship-development-90-P01642

Thomas, R. (2021, March 31). *What are the 5 stages of
puberty? The Tanner stages of puberty.* Amazing Me.
https://www.amazingme.com.au/what-are-the-
5-stages-of-puberty/

Tripple, M. (2021, February 13). *50 Life-changing quotes
for teenage girls.* Confessions of Parenting.
https://confessionsofparenting.com/quotes-
for-teenage-girls/

Turner, C., and Kamanetz, A. (2020, February 11).
What your teen wishes you knew about sex education.

NPR.
https://www.npr.org/2020/02/10/804508548
/what-your-teen-wishes-you-knew-about-sex-
education

Twersky, E., and Twersky, C. (2018, October 30). 7
Tips to rock your first date! *Seventeen.*
https://www.seventeen.com/love/dating-
advice/advice/a7582/first-date-tips/

200+ First date quotes. (2022, October 21). Happily
Lover. https://happilylover.com/first-date-
quotes/

Villines, Z. (2020, February 25). Should you clean your
vagina? *Medical News Today.*
https://www.medicalnewstoday.com/articles/h
ow-to-clean-your-vagina

WebMD Editorial Contributors. (2021, June 27). *What
is foreplay?* WebMD.
https://www.webmd.com/sex/what-is-foreplay

WebMD Editorial Contributors. (2022, February 6).
Teens and virginity. WebMD.
https://teens.webmd.com/teens-virginity

Weinstein, T. (2022, November 1). *Teenage love and
relationships: What parents can expect.* Newport
Academy.
https://www.newportacademy.com/resources/
empowering-teens/teenage-love/

What are pantyliners for? Are they good for you? (2023,
February 10). Flo.health.

https://flo.health/menstrual-cycle/lifestyle/hygiene-and-beauty/panty-liners

What to do if you're a teenager and pregnant: Your 3 options. (2017, August 7). Unplanned Pregnancy. https://unplannedpregnancy.com/facing-an-unplanned-pregnancy/age/teenage-unwanted-pregnancy/

Willis Aronowitz, N. (2019, June 6). How to get abortion if you're a teen. *Teen Vogue.* https://www.teenvogue.com/story/how-to-get-an-abortion-if-youre-a-teen

Winslow, A. (2021). *First date tips for teenagers! Dating tips for teens planning your first date* [Video]. On YouTube. https://www.youtube.com/watch?v=G9TZB1_u0DI

World Health Organization. (2023, January 31). *Female genital mutilation. WHO International.* https://www.who.int/news-room/fact-sheets/detail/female-genital-mutilation

Made in the USA
Las Vegas, NV
26 November 2023

81604020R00118